√M

D0383138

Mable Hoffman's FINGER FOODS

Co-authored by Gar Hoffman

a division of
PRICE STERN SLOAN
Los Angeles

Photography & Food Styling: Burke/Triolo

The following Los Angeles galleries provided tableware for photography: Geary's, Wilder Place, Freehand, New Stone Age, Lynn Deutch, Umbrello, Tesoro and The Pavilion at Tanner Market.

Library of Congress Cataloging-in-Publication Data

Hoffman, Mable.
    Finger Foods / by Mable Hoffman ; co-authored by Gar Hoffman.
        p.   cm.
    Includes index.
    ISBN 0-89586-664-1
    1. Cookery. I. Hoffman, Gar. II. Title.
TX714.H64 1989   1989-1661
641.5—dc   CIP

HPBooks, A division of Price Stern Sloan, Inc.
360 North La Cienega Boulevard, Los Angeles, California 90048
© 1989 HPBooks   Printed in the U.S.A.

10 9 8 7 6 5 4 3 2 1
77998

NOTICE: The information contained in this book is true and complete to the best of our knowledge. All recommendations are made without any guarantees on the part of the author or Price Stern Sloan. The author and publisher disclaim all liability in connection with the use of this information.

Cover photo: Pesto-Stuffed Cherry Tomatoes, page 131; Green 'n' Gold Walk-Away Salad, page 128; Skewered Szechuan-Style Barbecued Pork, page 125; White-Chocolate-Raspberry Cups, page 75; Chocolate-Buttercream Ladyfinger Sandwiches, page 81.

TABLE of CONTENTS

Acknowledgements

Special thanks to Jan Robertson for her overall assistance and recipe testing. Also thanks to Grace Wheeler for her special assistance, Retha M. Davis for her editorial work, and to Jeanette Egan for her overall coordination of this project on behalf of HPBooks.

Mable & Gar Hoffman's cookbook writings have been numerous including an unprecedented five R. T. French Tastemaker Awards, the "Oscar" for cookbooks. Numerous titles include *Make-Ahead Entertaining, California Cooking, Ice Cream, Chocolate Cookery, Appetizers, Deep-Fry Cookery, Crepe Cookery* and *Crockery Cookery*. In addition to their team-approach to writing, together they delight in entertaining, whether it be small or large groups, family or friends, or formal or casual. Nothing fits with entertaining better than the ease and simplicity of *Finger Foods*. With today's easy, casual lifestyle, the Hoffmans hope you enjoy preparing many finger foods, whether for everyday family needs, or for those special times on your calendar.

The Hoffmans also enjoy traveling and researching regional and ethnic cuisine. Throughout this book, you'll find delicious recipes they have created based on some of the foods they've enjoyed while visiting various parts of the world. Hoffman Food Consultants is their joint business, specializing in food styling, recipe development and general food consulting and writing.

Introduction

For those of us who, as children, dreamed of eating with our fingers, but were properly trained to use a knife and fork, the world has finally caught up with our fantasy.

Now, finger foods are not only socially acceptable, but are very popular at home, supermarkets, delicatessens and fast-food establishments.

This book is designed to enable you to enjoy these foods with your family, as well as at times when you're entertaining friends in a relaxed, informal manner.

What is a Finger Food?

A finger food is an individual serving, or food that can be easily cut or broken into a single serving. It should be small enough to be eaten without utensils. Ideally, it does not break, drip, crumble, mash, bend or disintegrate from the time it leaves the serving plate until it reaches your mouth. Sometimes we bend these rules and enjoy picking up a crumbly muffin, a drippy taco or a crusty drumstick. Although they are slightly messy, we overlook their shortcomings and continue to pick them up with our fingers.

Why Finger Foods Are Popular

- There's a more relaxed atmosphere when finger food is served. Casual eating results in a more comfortable feeling than knife and fork service.

- Finger foods are more practical for those in a hurry. Each person can pick up his food and eat it on-the-run.

- Families are no longer sticking to traditional dinner hours or "meat and potatoes" menus. Finger foods are more adaptable for different schedules.

- Children are more likely to pick up and taste unfamiliar foods, than to cut them with a knife and eat with a fork. The same principle applies to adults tasting new gourmet foods.

- Guests at a buffet or cocktail party are more mobile if they do not have to use silverware.

Current Food Trends That Encourage Finger Foods

- Interest in lighter foods encourages a variety of smaller, more nutritious servings. From a dietary point of view, this plan keeps you from feeling deprived from heavier, more calorie-laden foods.

- Many of the country's most prominent chefs feature a succession of appetizers, snacks and desserts on their menus instead of a traditional menu.

- A relaxing of rigid rules about set menus for each meal has occurred. There's no protocol about the kind of food or the way it is served.

- Restaurants and delis that feature take-out foods are selling a high percentage of finger foods.

- Sports fans are accustomed to snacking on finger foods throughout baseball and football games, as well as other events.

- Food manufacturers realize that we like easy-to-eat single servings or those that can be easily divided into individual portions. As a result, supermarkets are offering more and more choices.

- Our most popular ethnic foods fit into the finger-food category. Included are Spanish tapas, Chinese dim sum, Mexican tacos and many varieties of pizza.

- Fast-food establishments are the real leaders in this trend. Imagine the consumed volume of bite-sized chicken pieces, filled biscuits, fried shrimp, breakfast English muffins and French fries, in addition to the ever-popular burgers.

Tips for Making Finger Foods

- Make the most of all your equipment.
  Toaster Oven—This is a most practical small appliance for individual servings or small quantities. It's handy for making hot sandwiches, melting cheese and baking small tarts or cakes.
  Oven & Broiler—Use these for all kinds of baking and broiling with any recipe that's too large for a toaster oven.
  Electric Deep-Fryer—Follow the heating directions according to the manufacturer's instructions. Do not put food in hot oil until it reaches the proper temperature.
  Griddle & Sandwichmaker—These are handy for grilling sandwiches and tortillas.
  Freezer—Wrap individual servings of finger foods in freezer bags or freezer wrap. Store in a freezer; remove and thaw as needed.
  Microwave—This is a time-saving appliance for most finger foods. It's helpful in preparing recipes or heating individual foods when family members are on different schedules.

  Slow Cooker—Here's a practical way to keep foods hot at a buffet table or for a picnic. Prepare your favorite meatballs or cubes of poultry according to directions; then transfer them to a slow cooker to keep them warm. Have small wooden picks nearby for serving.
  Baking Pans—Some pans which are excellent for making finger foods include several sizes of muffin pans, custard cups, tart pans, small loaf pans and miniature quiche pans.

- Have your deli slice cheese and cold cuts to specifications in recipes. If you are in a hurry, buy ready-made salads or relishes to complete the menu.

- Save time by using refrigerator or frozen breads and rolls, tortillas, pita bread rounds or bakery rolls as the base for recipes.

- Take short-cuts with bottled dressings, taco sauce, teriyaki sauce and barbecue sauce.

Serving Suggestions

These recipe groupings are suggested combinations from *Finger Foods* for certain theme activities or types of meals. They are not complete menus, but rather recipes which might go well together depending on your personal tastes. Using your own favorite recipes as well as some ideas from this collection, you can create special menus for entertaining family, friends and all those special guests throughout the year.

A Trip to Tropical Paradise

Islandia Fish Kabobs, page 60
Maylasian Triangles, page 104
Crab-Stuffed Artichoke Bottoms, page 149
Hawaiian Cheese Tarts, page 76
Island Magic Cakes, page 90
Hawaiian Popcorn, pages 112-113
Tropical Stacks, page 139
Seashell Madeleine Cookies, page 140
Tropical-Fruit Kabobs, pages 22-23 and 25

Backyard Barbecue

Mediterranean Barbecued Burgers, page 123
Garden-Path Dip for Pita Wedges, page 67
Green 'n' Gold Walk-Away Salad, page 128
S'Mores Bars, page 109
Sunset Pops, pages 106-108

Bridge Club Luncheon

California Quiche, pages 30-31
Layered Tuna-Egg Loaf, page 43
Pesto-Stuffed Cherry Tomatoes, page 131
White-Chocolate-Raspberry Cups, page 75
   and cover

Guys Night Together

Barbecued Beef on a Bun, page 42
Oriental-Style Baby-Back Ribs, page 62
Smoky Cheese-Potato Slices, page 66
Roquefort-Onion Rolls, page 71
Praline Squares, page 83

Teen Night

Pizza Rolls, page 35
Munchy Sesame Wings, page 58
Chunky Herbed Bread Sticks, page 70
Butterscotch-Macaroon Ice-Cream Sandwich,
   page 108

School Lunch Box

Short-Cut Soft Pretzel, page 117,
   with cheese spread
Crunchy Granola Bar, page 12

Harvest Festival

All-American Turkey Meatballs, page 100
Cold Meat Party Carousel, page 149
Crumb-Coated Zucchini Diagonals, page 66
Pumpkin-Pecan Bread, page 32
Apple-Spice Diagonals, page 82

A Chocoholic's Dream Party

Double Chocolate-Pecan Treats, page 144
Peanutty-Chocolate Popcorn Clusters,
   pages 113-114
Rocky-Road Cheesecake Cups, page 78
Mississippi Mud Bars, page 83
Chocolate-Cashew Baklava Wrap-Ups, page 87
Chocolate-Almond Truffles, page 111

Shower Luncheon

Roquefort Tortas, page 45 with
  apple slices, orange segments, green grapes
Chocolate-Buttercream Ladyfinger Sandwiches,
  page 81

South-of-the-Border

Mexican Pork Cubes, page 103
Smoked-Sausage Burritos, page 28
Bean-Tortilla Crisp, page 52
Jalapeño Corn Muffins, page 68
South-of-the-Border Churros, page 115

Orient Express

Chicken-Mushroom Spring Rolls, page 46
Gingered Shrimp Balls, pages 98-99
Sesame-Crab Dumplings, pages 98-99
Won-Ton Treats, page 116

Children's Party

Smoky Canoes, page 37
Crunchy Corn-Dogs on a Stick, page 42
Tic-Tac-Toe Twists, page 152
Frozen Peanut-Butter Horns, page 86
Peanut Butter 'n' Jelly Ravioli Cookies, page 85

Family Reunion Picnic

Shangri-La Drumsticks, pages 123 and 129
Vegetable-Cheese Pita Pickups, page 131
Banana-Fruit Chews, page 84

Birthday Tea

Herbed Party Sandwiches, pages 146-147
Double Salmon Pinwheels, pages 92-94
Apricot-Cheesecake Muffins, page 33
Tropical-Fruit Kabobs, pages 22-23 and 25
Royal Viking Almond Cookies, page 85
Seashell Madeleine Cookies, page 140

Brunch with Friends

Sausage-Stuffed Mushrooms, page 26
California Quiche, pages 30-31
Herb-Parmesan Muffins, pages 68-69
Apple-Cheese Brunch Wedges, page 27
Duo-Dip Fruit Platter, page 24

Holiday Gift Ideas

Orange-Spiced Nuts, page 110
Spiced Fruit & Nut Clusters, page 111
Hawaiian Popcorn, pages 112-113
Ranch 'n' Surf Munchies, page 116
Tropical Stacks, page 139
Orange-Mincemeat Loaf, page 141
Cranberry-White-Chocolate Cereal Bars,
  page 142
Pumpkin-Pecan Bread, page 32
Spicy Holiday Thumbprints, page 141

Italian Buffet

Layered Pesto Spread, page 148
Sicilian Prosciutto Roll-Arounds, page 95
Parma Eggs, page 132
Walk-Away Italian Salad, page 53
Neopolitan Slices, page 104
Sicilian Chocolate-Pistachio Cannolis, page 91

Breakfast on the Go

Breakfast is the meal when most everyone is watching the clock. Often it is skipped entirely due to oversleeping or early morning commitments. We designed this chapter to give in-a-hurry sleepyheads ideas for eating on the way to work or school.

We suggest that you take advantage of prepared time-saving breads, such as refrigerator biscuits and rolls, rice cakes, pita bread, English muffins and tortillas. If necessary, make up toppings the night before. Peanutty Rice Cakes have a nutritious combination of peanut butter plus dried and fresh fruits. For a super speedy breakfast, spread this mixture on a rice cake; then pick it up and enjoy it on your way. If you have a few additional minutes for breakfast, you'll enjoy Pita Bread Breakfast Rounds. They are made with pita bread topped with eggs, ham, cheese, tomato and avocado. A few more minutes of preparation will result in Ham 'n' Egg Muffin Cups.

It's hard to beat the natural flavors of fresh fruits for breakfast. They're nature's original finger foods. When the vines and trees are laden with a bountiful harvest, eat them "as is," or cut pears, peaches, apples, oranges and nectarines into wedges or halves, for ease in eating on-the-go.

Quick Menus

Sausage & Egg to Go
Orange Wedges
Hot Chocolate

Cream-Cheese & Lox Pâté
Seedless grapes
Coffee

Cream-Cheese & Lox Pâté

An updated version of an ever-popular combination, but with more complex flavors. Prepare pâté the night before, refrigerate and it's ready to spread on bagels for breakfast.
(Photo on previous pages.)

1 (8-oz.) package cream cheese with herbs and garlic
1/4 cup plain yogurt
1 tablespoon finely chopped fresh parsley
1/4 teaspoon grated lemon peel

1 tablespoon finely chopped green onion
4 ounces thinly sliced smoked salmon (lox), chopped
1/2 teaspoon Dijon-style mustard
4 to 6 bagels, sliced

In a medium bowl, combine cream cheese and yogurt. Stir in parsley, lemon peel, green onion, salmon and mustard. Serve now or cover and refrigerate. Spread cut-side of each bagel with pâté. Makes about 1-1/2 cups pâté.

Crunchy Granola Bars

Make these bars on the weekend. Store in a covered container so they'll be fresh and ready for breakfast throughout the week. Or, take an extra bar for a mid-morning break or lunch.

3/4 cup lightly packed brown sugar
1/2 cup butter or margarine, room temperature
2 eggs
1/2 teaspoon baking soda
1 teaspoon vanilla extract
1 teaspoon ground cinnamon
1 cup all-purpose flour

1-1/2 cups regular or quick-cooking rolled oats
1/2 cup chopped peanuts
1/2 cup raisins
1/2 cup flaked coconut
1/4 cup shelled sunflower seeds
4 ounces semisweet chocolate, optional
1 tablespoon butter or margarine, optional

Preheat oven to 350F (175C). Grease a 13" x 9" baking pan. In a large bowl, cream brown sugar and 1/2 cup butter. Add eggs; beat until light and fluffy. Beat in baking soda, vanilla, cinnamon and flour. Stir in rolled oats, peanuts, raisins, coconut and sunflower seeds. Firmly press mixture into bottom of greased pan. Bake in preheated oven 20 to 25 minutes or until set. Remove from oven; cool on a rack. When cool, cut into 2-inch bars. If chocolate coating is desired, combine chocolate and 1 tablespoon butter in a small pan. Stir over low heat until melted. Spoon chocolate mixture over one end of each bar. Let stand until chocolate is firm. Makes about 24 bars.

Healthy Breakfast Spread

When you oversleep or are short on time, spread this mixture on a muffin or bagel, omit the broiling and devour it on your way to school or work.

1/4 cup peanut butter
1 tablespoon honey
1/2 cup drained tofu
1 banana, mashed

1/4 teaspoon grated orange peel
5 English muffins, split, toasted
Ground cinnamon

In a small bowl, combine peanut butter, honey, tofu, banana and orange peel; blend well. Spread mixture on cut side of toasted English-muffin halves. Sprinkle with cinnamon. Broil 4 to 5 inches from heat source until bubbly. Makes about 1 cup spread.

Graham Cracker Pickups

To avoid last-minute preparation, make the spread ahead of time; then cover and refrigerate until serving time. To serve, spread on graham crackers and enjoy!

1/4 cup trail mix
1/4 cup canned crushed pineapple, drained
2 tablespoons chopped walnuts

1/4 cup (2 oz.) ricotta cheese
2 teaspoons honey
8 graham-cracker squares

In a small bowl, combine trail mix, pineapple, walnuts, ricotta cheese and honey. Spread on graham crackers. Serve immediately. Makes 8 servings.

Breakfast Burrito

When cooking egg mixture, gently lift cooked area, letting uncooked liquid flow under cooked egg.

2 eggs, beaten slightly
1 teaspoon canned diced green chilies
1/2 teaspoon finely chopped green onion
1 tablespoon chopped ham or crumbled cooked
   bacon
1 tablespoon water

1/8 teaspoon salt
1 teaspoon butter or margarine
1 tablespoon shredded Monterey Jack cheese
1 (8-inch) flour tortilla
2 tablespoons refried beans
1 teaspoon dairy sour cream

In a small bowl, combine eggs, chilies, green onion, ham or bacon, water and salt. In a 7-inch skillet or omelet pan, melt butter. Pour in egg mixture. Cook eggs to desired consistency. Remove from heat; sprinkle with cheese. Preheat a skillet or griddle. Place tortilla on preheated skillet or griddle; quickly turn tortilla, heating other side long enough to soften. Or, heat tortilla in a plastic bag in a microwave on high 5 to 8 seconds. Slide cooked eggs onto warm tortilla. Top with beans and sour cream. Roll up and eat while warm. Makes 1 serving.

Smoked-Sausage Muffin Cups

Layers of dough with ingredients between, stand on end like the ever-popular butterflake rolls.

1 (8-oz.) package refrigerator crescent rolls
1 tablespoon finely chopped green onion
1/2 cup (2 oz.) grated Cheddar cheese
1/4 teaspoon ground sage

2 or 3 drops hot-pepper sauce
2 ounces Kielbasa or smoked sausage, cut into 16
   thin slices

Preheat oven to 400F (205C). Grease 8 (2-1/2- to 3-inch) muffin cups. Unroll crescent-roll dough. Divide dough into 2 rectangles with 4 triangles in each. With fingers, press out perforations. With a large sharp knife, cut each rectangle lengthwise in half; then cut each half into 6 (2-inch) squares, making a total of 24 squares. In a small bowl, combine green onion, cheese, sage and hot-pepper sauce. Place 1 slice of sausage and about 1 tablespoon cheese mixture on each of 8 dough squares. Top each with another square of dough, another slice of sausage and some cheese mixture; top each with a third square of dough. Place each dough stack on end in a prepared muffin cup. Bake in preheated oven 10 minutes or until bread is golden. Remove from oven. Cool about 5 minutes. Loosen from sides; remove from pan. Serve warm. Makes 8 servings.

Breakfast on the Run

*To sleepyheads: pick up one of these "portable breakfasts" and
eat it en route to your workplace.*

4 (4-inch) French rolls
3 ounces cream cheese, room temperature
1 teaspoon Dijon-style mustard
1/2 cup (2-1/2 oz.) chopped cooked ham
1 tablespoon butter or margarine

4 eggs
2 tablespoons milk
1/4 teaspoon salt
1/8 teaspoon pepper
1 tablespoon chopped chives for garnish

Preheat oven to 375F (190C). Slice off top of each roll about 1/2 inch from top. Scoop out center of each roll, leaving about 1/2 inch around sides and bottom. Use scooped out crumbs for another purpose. In a small bowl, combine cream cheese and mustard. Spread mixture in bottom of each scooped-out roll. Sprinkle rolls with ham; cover with tops of rolls. Place in a shallow baking pan. Bake in preheated oven 7 to 8 minutes. In a medium skillet, melt butter. In a medium bowl, beat together eggs, milk, salt and pepper. Pour egg mixture into hot skillet; stir gently, cooking to desired consistency. Remove tops of rolls; spoon cooked eggs into heated ham-filled rolls. Sprinkle lightly with chopped chives. Replace tops. Serve warm. Makes 4 servings.

Sausage & Egg to Go

*Mustard enthusiasts will like to spread their favorite mustard inside
each pita bread before adding sausage and eggs.*

3 ounces smoked sausage links, sliced
4 eggs, beaten slightly
1/4 cup dairy sour cream
1/2 teaspoon Worcestershire sauce

2 teaspoons finely chopped chives
1/8 teaspoon pepper
2 (6-inch) pita bread rounds, halved crosswise

In an 8-inch skillet over medium heat, cook sliced sausage until lightly browned. Remove from pan; drain on paper towels. In a medium bowl, combine eggs, sour cream, Worcestershire sauce, chives and pepper. Pour egg mixture into hot skillet; add cooked sausage. Stir gently, cooking until egg mixture is firm but still moist. Spoon mixture into each pita bread half. Makes 4 stuffed pita bread halves.

Breakfast Biscuit Cups

*Small cans of refrigerated biscuits contain five or six; either
amount works with this recipe.*

1 (4.5- or 5-oz.) package refrigerated biscuits
1/2 cup chopped boiled or baked ham
2 eggs, beaten slightly

2 tablespoons dairy sour cream
1/8 teaspoon seasoned salt
1/2 cup (2 oz.) shredded Cheddar cheese

Preheat oven to 400F (205C). On a lightly floured board, roll out each biscuit to a 5-inch circle. Press each rolled biscuit into a 10-ounce baking cup. Sprinkle ham over each biscuit. In a small bowl, combine eggs, sour cream and seasoned salt. Spoon evenly over ham. Top with cheese. Bake in preheated oven 15 minutes or until golden brown. Serve warm. Makes 5 or 6 servings.

Ham 'n' Egg Muffin Cups

*Let the Ham 'n' Egg Cups bake while you're getting ready for work
or school. Then, if you're pressed for time, eat them on the run.*

4 (4-inch-square) thin slices boiled or baked ham
1 medium tomato, cut into 4 slices
4 eggs
Salt

Pepper
1/3 cup (1-1/2 oz.) shredded Swiss cheese
2 English muffins, split, toasted

Preheat oven to 375F (190C). Line 4 (4-inch) tart or quiche pans with ham slices. Top each with a slice of tomato. Drop 1 uncooked egg over each tomato slice. Sprinkle with salt, pepper and cheese. Bake in preheated oven 15 minutes or until eggs reach desired consistency. Slide one cooked ham cup onto each English-muffin half. Makes 4 servings.

Pita Bread Breakfast Rounds

Put your complete breakfast in a pita bread round.

2 (6-inch) pita bread rounds
2 tablespoons butter or margarine
4 eggs
2 tablespoons milk
1/4 teaspoon salt
1/8 teaspoon pepper

1 teaspoon chopped chives
4 thin slices ham
1/2 cup (2 oz.) shredded Cheddar cheese
1 medium tomato, cut into 4 slices, for garnish
1 avocado, sliced, for garnish

Carefully split each pita bread to form 2 thin rounds. In a medium skillet, melt butter. In a small bowl, beat together eggs, milk, salt and pepper; stir in chives. Pour egg mixture into hot skillet; stir gently, cooking until set but slightly underdone. Place 1 slice of ham on each pita bread half; top with cooked eggs. Sprinkle 2 tablespoons cheese over each. Broil 4 to 5 inches from heat source 2 minutes or until cheese melts. Garnish with tomato and avocado slices. Makes 4 servings.

Smoky Cheese Muffins

A quick and easy treat with a tantalizing smoky flavor.

1 cup (4 oz.) shredded smoked Gouda cheese
1 tablespoon finely chopped chives
1 tablespoon finely chopped fresh parsley
1/4 cup mayonnaise

2 slices bacon, cooked, crumbled
1/2 teaspoon Worcestershire sauce
4 English muffins, split

In a small bowl, combine cheese, chives, parsley, mayonnaise, bacon and Worcestershire sauce. Spread about 2 tablespoons cheese mixture on each muffin half. Place muffin halves on a baking sheet. Broil 3 to 4 inches from heat source 2 to 3 minutes or until bubbly. Makes 8 muffin halves.

Maple-Glazed Apples on Raisin Toast

*A few minutes of cooking time is well spent when the result is
such a delicious combination of flavors. This is one of our favorite
pickup breakfasts.*

2 medium apples

2 tablespoons butter or margarine

2 tablespoons maple syrup

4 slices raisin bread, toasted

1/2 cup whipped cream cheese

3 tablespoons chopped pecans, optional

Core apples; cut each into 8 wedges. In a medium skillet, heat butter and maple syrup until butter melts. Add apple wedges; cook over low heat until one side is glazed. Turn and glaze other side. Spread each slice of toast with about 2 tablespoons whipped cream cheese. Top each with 4 glazed apple wedges. Sprinkle with chopped pecans, if desired. Makes 4 servings.

Fruity Ricotta-Almond Toast

*This is a quick way to have fruit and toast at the same time.
Refrigerate the spread for several days for a fast toast topping.*

1 cup (8 oz.) ricotta cheese

2 tablespoons toasted slivered almonds

2 tablespoons honey

1/8 teaspoon ground cardamom

8 slices bread, toasted

4 nectarines or peaches, sliced

In a blender or food processor fitted with the metal blade, combine ricotta cheese, almonds, honey and cardamom. Process until almost smooth. Spread about 2 tablespoons cheese mixture on each slice of toast. Top with sliced nectarines or peaches. Makes 8 servings.

Scandinavian Cheese Rounds

The favorite Norwegian cheese called **gjetost,** *transforms plain
rice cakes into a special treat.*

1 cup (4 oz.) shredded gjetost cheese
1 (3-oz.) package cream cheese, room
   temperature
1 tablespoon dairy sour cream

2 tablespoons chopped pecans
4 rice cakes
Ground nutmeg

In a small bowl, combine gjetost, cream cheese, sour cream and pecans. Spread cheese mixture on rice cakes. Sprinkle lightly with nutmeg. Makes 4 servings.

Peanutty Rice Cakes

*Packages of dried fruit morsels usually contain apricots, peaches,
apples and raisins. Make your own combination by chopping your
favorite dried fruits into 1/4-inch pieces. Add raisins, if desired.*

1/2 cup crunchy peanut butter
1/4 cup dried fruit morsels
1 small apple, peeled, shredded

6 rice cakes
2 tablespoons dried fruit morsels

In a small bowl, combine peanut butter, 1/4 cup dried fruit morsels and shredded apple. Spread mixture on rice cakes. Sprinkle additional dried fruit morsels on top for garnish. Makes 6 servings.

Good Morning Foldovers

*By using a 10- to 12-inch skillet, you can brown two filled tortillas
at a time.*

1/2 pound hot Italian sausage	4 (8-inch) flour tortillas
1/4 cup chopped green onions	1/4 cup (3/4 oz.) grated Parmesan cheese
2 eggs, beaten slightly	2 tablespoons vegetable oil

Remove casing from sausage. In a small skillet, cook sausage, crumbling it with a fork as it cooks; drain well. Sprinkle about 1/4 cup cooked sausage, 1 tablespoon green onion and 2 tablespoons beaten egg over 1/2 of a flour tortilla. Sprinkle with 1 tablespoon cheese. Fold tortilla in half, enclosing ingredients. Repeat with remaining ingredients and tortillas. Heat oil in a large skillet. Fry filled tortillas until golden on each side. Makes 4 servings.

Bagel Cartwheels

*Enjoy these crispy bagels alone or use them as a base for cream
cheese or your favorite cheese spread.*

3 bagels	1/4 teaspoon smoked salt
3 tablespoons butter or margarine, melted	

Preheat oven to 300F (155C). With a sharp knife, split each bagel into 4 thin cartwheels. Brush each with melted butter; sprinkle with smoked salt. Place seasoned bagels in a 15" x 10" jelly-roll pan. Bake in preheated oven 25 minutes or until crisp and light golden color. Serve warm or cool. Makes 12 cartwheels.

Variation
For a simple party snack, use miniature cocktail bagels and follow directions as above.

Finger-Licking Brunches

Brunch is the best of both worlds. It's appropriate to serve foods traditionally associated with breakfast, as well as those that are usually on the lunch menu. Many restaurants, realizing the interest in brunch, have established their reputation on Sunday brunch.

For home entertaining, brunch is popular because it is informal and easy on the budget. Best of all, the menu can be very flexible and easy to prepare. There are no rigid rules. You can offer wonderful homemade hot breads, like Apricot-Cheesecake Muffins, or show off your culinary expertise with Pizza Rolls that have all the irresistible ingredients of the best pizza in town.

If eggs are your choice, you'll like English-Muffin Orange French Toast. Egg-Muffin Crowns also use English muffins as a base for sliced turkey and eggs that are smothered in a combination of Roquefort dressing and Monterey Jack cheese. For a south-of-the-border finger food, try Baja Blintzes. They are tortillas filled with ham and eggs that are enhanced by a slightly spicy sauce.

To complete the brunch menu, you'll want to add seasonal fresh fruits and your favorite beverage.

Prosciutto-Stuffed Fresh Figs

*Use this idea during the short season for fresh figs. They're a real
conversation piece when featured on a fresh-fruit tray.*

3 tablespoons finely chopped prosciutto

1/3 cup (3 oz.) ricotta cheese

1 teaspoon honey

1/2 teaspoon sweet-hot mustard

1 teaspoon finely chopped crystallized ginger

6 to 8 fresh figs

In a small bowl, combine prosciutto, ricotta cheese, honey, mustard and ginger. Remove stems from figs. Make an "X" cut from top almost to bottom of each fig. Spoon about 1 tablespoon filling into center of each fig. Serve immediately or cover and refrigerate up to 24 hours. Makes 6 to 8 stuffed figs.

Duo-Dip Fruit Platter

*Choose between the slightly sweet strawberry dip or the more
savory cheese spread with a European flavor.*

2 apples, cored, thinly sliced

2 pears, cored, thinly sliced

2 tangerines, peeled, sectioned

1 papaya, peeled, sliced

1 large bunch seedless grapes

Arrange fruit on a large tray. Serve with Creamy Strawberry-Almond Dip or Mediterranean Cheese Spread. Makes 8 to 10 servings.

Creamy Strawberry-Almond Dip:

3/4 cup strawberry yogurt

1/2 cup non-dairy whipped topping

2 tablespoons finely chopped toasted almonds

In a small bowl, combine yogurt and non-dairy topping. Sprinkle with toasted almonds. Makes 1-1/4 cups.

Mediterranean Cheese Spread:

1 (8-oz.) package Neufchâtel cheese, room temperature

2 ounces prosciutto, finely chopped   (7 or 8 very thin slices)

1/3 cup dairy sour cream

2 tablespoons crumbled Roquefort cheese

In small bowl, combine Neufchâtel cheese, prosciutto, sour cream and Roquefort cheese. Makes about 1-2/3 cups.

Tropical-Fruit Kabobs

*An eye-appealing way to entice your family or guests to enjoy
fresh fruits. (Photo on pages 22-23.)*

8 ounces apricot-pineapple yogurt
1 tablespoon finely chopped crystallized ginger
1/4 cup flaked coconut
1 teaspoon honey
1/4 teaspoon grated orange peel

2 kiwi fruit
1 large orange
1 banana
8 strawberries

In a small bowl, combine yogurt, ginger, coconut, honey and orange peel. Refrigerate at least 1 hour. Peel kiwi fruit; cut each into quarters lengthwise. Peel orange; cut into 4 thick crosswise slices. Cut each slice in half. Peel banana; cut into 8 chunks. Thread fruits alternately on 8 (6-inch) wooden skewers, ending each with a strawberry. Dip each kabob in chilled yogurt mixture. Serve immediately. Makes 8 servings.

Korean Omelet Wrap-Ups

*These are very thin pickup omelets. The vegetable filling was
inspired by a Korean recipe. We like tortillas with it, so decided to
use them as wrappers.*

1 tablespoon vegetable oil
2 teaspoons sesame oil
1 small zucchini, cut into 2-inch matchsticks
1/2 of a large red bell pepper, cut into 2-inch
   matchsticks
1 jalapeño pepper, seeded, finely chopped
2 tablespoons thinly sliced green onion

1/4 teaspoon salt
1/2 cup bean sprouts
6 eggs, beaten slightly
2 tablespoons soy sauce
2 tablespoons butter or margarine
4 (8-inch) flour tortillas, warmed

In an 8- or 9-inch skillet, heat vegetable oil and sesame oil. Add zucchini, red bell pepper, jalapeño pepper and green onion. Cook until vegetables are soft but not completely done. Stir in salt and bean sprouts. Remove from heat; cool slightly. In a medium bowl, combine eggs, soy sauce and cooked vegetables. Melt 1/2 tablespoon butter in skillet. Spoon one-fourth the vegetable-egg mixture into skillet. Evenly spread out vegetables with back of a spoon. Cook over medium-low heat until golden on both sides. Repeat with remaining butter and vegetable-egg mixture. Place a cooked vegetable omelet on each warm tortilla. Roll up; serve immediately. Makes 4 servings.

Bouillon-Cheese Toast

*Tried and true French toast was never like this! Bouillon and
cheese put it into a different category.*

1 teaspoon chicken bouillon granules or
   1 bouillon cube, crumbled
2 tablespoons warm water
2 eggs, beaten slightly
1 teaspoon Worcestershire sauce

Dash hot-pepper sauce
2 tablespoons butter or margarine
6 slices bread
2 tablespoons grated Parmesan cheese

In a shallow, medium bowl, dissolve bouillon in water. Add eggs, Worcestershire sauce and hot-pepper sauce. In a 10-inch skillet, melt 1 tablespoon butter. Dip 3 slices bread in egg mixture, then place in hot skillet; brown on both sides. Immediately sprinkle bread with 1/2 the Parmesan cheese. Cut in halves or quarters to serve. Repeat with remaining butter, egg mixture, bread and cheese. Serve warm. Makes 12 half-slices or 24 quarters.

Sausage-Stuffed Mushrooms

Save mushroom stems to enhance a salad, stew or soup.

1/2 pound bulk pork sausage
2 tablespoons finely chopped onion
1 teaspoon finely chopped fresh parsley
1/8 teaspoon salt
1/8 teaspoon pepper

1 egg, beaten slightly
1/2 cup soft bread crumbs
16 to 18 large mushrooms (1-1/2- to 1-3/4-inch)
2 tablespoons grated Parmesan cheese

Preheat oven to 350F (175C). In a small skillet, combine sausage and onion. Cook over medium heat, breaking up sausage with a fork while cooking. Remove from heat; drain well. Stir in parsley, salt, pepper, egg and bread crumbs. Remove stems from mushrooms; use for another purpose. Spoon sausage mixture into mushroom caps, mounding each slightly. Place stuffed mushrooms in a shallow baking pan. Sprinkle stuffed mushrooms with Parmesan cheese. Bake in preheated oven 8 to 10 minutes. Serve hot. Makes 16 to 18 stuffed mushrooms.

English-Muffin Orange French Toast

Let the muffins soak in egg mixture so they can absorb the orange flavor.

3 eggs, beaten slightly
1/3 cup orange juice
1/4 teaspoon grated orange peel
1 tablespoon milk
1/4 teaspoon salt
1/16 teaspoon pepper

3 English muffins, split
2 tablespoons butter or margarine
Powdered sugar
6 large strawberries, halved
1 papaya, peeled, sliced

In a 13" x 9" baking dish, combine eggs, orange juice, orange peel, milk, salt and pepper. Place muffin halves, cut-side up, in egg mixture; cover and refrigerate 10 minutes. Turn muffins cut-side down in mixture; cover and refrigerate at least 1 hour. In a large skillet or griddle, melt butter. Place egg-soaked muffins, cut-side up, in hot butter. Cook until golden brown. Turn and brown other side. Cut each muffin half in half again resulting in 12 half-circle pieces. Sprinkle each with powdered sugar; top with a strawberry half and a slice of papaya. Makes 12 half-circles of French toast.

Apple-Cheese Brunch Wedges

This tastes wonderful anytime, but is easier to cut into wedges if it stands at least 10 minutes after baking.

1/2 cup butter or margarine, room temperature
2/3 cup sugar
2 eggs
1/2 cup plain yogurt
1/2 teaspoon baking powder
1/4 teaspoon baking soda
1/4 teaspoon salt

2 cups all-purpose flour
1 large cooking apple, peeled, shredded
1/2 cup (2 oz.) shredded Swiss cheese
1/2 cup chopped toasted almonds
2 tablespoons sugar
1/8 teaspoon ground nutmeg

Preheat oven to 350F (175C). Grease a 9-inch springform pan. In a large bowl, cream butter and 2/3 cup sugar; beat in eggs and yogurt. Add baking powder, baking soda, salt and flour; beat just until well blended. Stir in apple, cheese and almonds. Spoon into prepared pan. Bake in preheated oven 35 to 40 minutes or until top springs back when touched with your finger tip. Remove from oven. In a small bowl, combine 2 tablespoons sugar and nutmeg; sprinkle on top of baked cake. Let stand 10 minutes. Cut into wedges. Serve warm or at room temperature. Makes 1 (9-inch) cake.

Variation
To use an 8-inch springform pan, reduce oven temperature to 325F (163C). Bake 40 to 50 minutes or until cake tests done.

Confetti Polenta Cups

*They aren't difficult to make, but be sure to pour the cornmeal in
very slowly to ensure a smooth mixture.*

1-1/4 cups chicken stock or bouillon
1/2 cup yellow cornmeal
1/4 cup chopped red bell pepper
2 tablespoons chopped green onion
1 teaspoon Dijon-style mustard
1/2 teaspoon salt

1/8 teaspoon pepper
3/4 cup (3 oz.) shredded Cheddar cheese
2 eggs, beaten slightly
1/2 cup dairy sour cream
Chopped red bell pepper for garnish
Chopped green onion for garnish

Preheat oven to 350F (175C). Grease 24 miniature muffin cups. In a medium saucepan, bring stock to a boil. Gradually pour in cornmeal, stirring constantly. Cook, stirring constantly, over medium heat 4 minutes or until very thick. Remove from heat. Stir in 1/4 cup bell pepper, 2 tablespoons green onion, mustard, salt, pepper and 1/2 cup cheese. In a small bowl, combine eggs and sour cream; stir into cooked cornmeal mixture. Spoon mixture into prepared muffin cups. Sprinkle with remaining 1/4 cup cheese. Bake in preheated oven 20 minutes or until firm. Remove from oven. Let stand about 5 minutes. Loosen from sides; remove from pans. Garnish with additional chopped red bell pepper and green onion, if desired. Serve warm. Makes 24 servings.

Smoked-Sausage Burritos

*Smoked-sausage links are just the right size for a burrito, and they
offer a nice flavor change from traditional ingredients.*

6 smoked-sausage links (about 9 oz.)
6 (8-inch) flour tortillas, warmed
3/4 cup refried beans
2 tablespoons chopped onion

2 tablespoons green-chili salsa or picante sauce
2/3 cup (3 oz.) grated Cheddar cheese
1 tablespoon vegetable oil
Salsa for dipping, optional

Preheat oven to 400F (205C). Split each sausage lengthwise, almost cutting it in half. Place a sausage on a warmed tortilla. Gently open sausage, being careful not to tear. Spoon about 2 tablespoons refried beans down center of split sausage. Top with onion and salsa. Sprinkle with cheese. Fold in ends of tortilla; roll up. Place in a shallow pan. Repeat with remaining sausages, tortillas and other ingredients. Brush each burrito with oil. Bake in preheated oven 15 to 20 minutes or until tortillas begin to brown. Serve warm with extra salsa for dipping, if desired. Makes 6 servings.

Brown & Serve Deviled Ham Rolls

A well-liked combination for anytime of day.

1/2 pound lean, smoked ham, cut into 1-inch
  pieces
1/2 cup chopped onion
3 tablespoons Dijon-style mustard
3 tablespoons mayonnaise
1/2 teaspoon pepper

1/8 teaspoon ground allspice
4 oz. Swiss cheese, cut into 1-inch pieces
12 unbaked brown-and-serve rolls
1 egg white
1 teaspoon water
Poppy seeds or caraway seeds for garnish

Preheat oven to 400F (205C). In a food processor fitted with the metal blade, combine ham, onion, mustard, mayonnaise, pepper and allspice. Process with on/off technique until ham is ground. With motor running, add cheese; process until cheese is grated. Make 3 even vertical cuts to within 1/4 inch of bottom of each roll. Spread 2 teaspoons ham mixture between each slice. Press together to reshape roll. Place each filled roll in an ungreased 2-1/2- to 3-inch muffin cup. In a small bowl, combine egg white and water. Brush tops of filled rolls with egg-white mixture. Sprinkle rolls with seeds. Bake in preheated oven 6 minutes or until golden brown. Serve warm. Makes 12 rolls.

Baja Blintzes

Popular flavors from south of the border are combined with
all-American ingredients.

2 tablespoons butter or margarine
3 tablespoons all-purpose flour
1/2 cup chicken stock or bouillon
1 cup milk or half and half
1 teaspoon grated onion
2 tablespoons canned diced green chilies

1/4 teaspoon salt
1/2 cup (2 oz.) shredded Monterey Jack cheese
3 hard-cooked eggs, sliced
1/2 cup chopped cooked ham
6 (8-inch) flour tortillas

Preheat oven to 375F (190C). In a small saucepan, melt butter. Stir in flour. Cook and stir 2 minutes. Stir in stock and milk. Cook, stirring constantly, over medium heat until thickened; remove from heat. Stir in onion, chilies, salt and cheese. Arrange 1/2 a sliced egg and 1 rounded tablespoon ham on each tortilla. Spoon about 2 tablespoons cheese sauce over ham. Fold both sides of each tortilla over filling; then fold top and bottom to slightly overlap in center. Place filled tortillas, folded-side down, in a shallow baking pan. Cover with foil. Bake in preheated oven 10 to 12 minutes or until heated through. Serve warm. Makes 6 servings.

California Quiche

Eye appealing mini-quiches using familiar flavors dressed up in pastry for a special look. Handy for almost any occasion from brunch to midnight snacks.

Pastry for a double-crust 9-inch pie
3 eggs, beaten slightly
1 cup dairy sour cream
3 tablespoons canned diced green chilies
1/2 cup sliced ripe olives
1/4 cup sliced green onions

1-1/2 cups (6 oz.) shredded Monterey Jack cheese
1/4 teaspoon salt
1/8 teaspoon pepper
Dairy sour cream for garnish
Sliced green onion for garnish

Preheat oven to 375F (190C). On a lightly floured board, roll out pastry to a 16" x 12" rectangle. Cut pastry into 12 (4-inch) circles. Ease each pastry circle into bottom and side of a 3-inch quiche pan or 4-inch tart pan. Trim pastry even with top of each pan. Arrange pans on a large baking sheet. In a medium bowl, combine eggs and 1 cup sour cream. Stir in chilies, olives, 1/4 cup green onions, cheese, salt and pepper. Spoon about 1/4 cup filling into each unbaked pastry shell. Bake in preheated oven 25 minutes or until filling is set. Remove from oven; let stand about 5 minutes. Loosen from sides; remove from pans. Garnish with additional sour cream and green onion. Serve warm or at room temperature. Makes 12 (3- to 4-inch) quiches.

Leek-Bacon Rounds

Fun to serve as an accompaniment to salads or with eggs for a special brunch.

1/2 pound lean bacon, diced
1 leek, washed, finely chopped
1 egg, separated
2 tablespoons water

1-3/4 cups all-purpose flour
1 teaspoon baking powder
1 tablespoon milk
Coarse salt or grated Parmesan cheese

Preheat oven to 375F (190C). In a medium skillet, sauté bacon until almost done. Add leek; cook until transparent. In a small bowl, beat egg white and water until blended. In a large bowl, combine flour and baking powder. Stir in egg-white mixture and bacon mixture with pan drippings. Stir with a fork until mixture forms a ball. Divide mixture into 24 (1-1/2-inch) balls. Arrange 12 balls on a baking sheet. With fingers, flatten each ball to a 2-1/2-inch circle. In a small bowl, beat egg yolk with milk. Brush top of circles with egg-yolk mixture. Sprinkle each round with coarse salt or cheese. Bake in preheated oven 12 to 14 minutes or until golden. Remove from oven; cool on a rack. Repeat with remaining balls as directed above. Makes 24 rounds.

◆

Orange-Coconut Puffs

This recipe makes six generous muffins. To serve a larger number of people, bake in miniature muffin pans.

1/4 cup vegetable shortening
1/3 cup sugar
1 egg
2/3 cup milk
1-1/4 cups all-purpose flour
1-1/4 teaspoons baking powder
1/4 teaspoon salt

1/2 teaspoon grated orange peel
1/4 cup flaked coconut
1 teaspoon finely chopped crystallized ginger
1/4 cup sugar
1/4 teaspoon ground nutmeg
1/3 cup butter or margarine, melted

Preheat oven to 400F (205C). Grease 6 (2-1/2- to 3-inch) muffin cups. In a medium bowl, cream shortening and 1/3 cup sugar; beat in egg and milk. Stir in flour, baking powder, salt, orange peel, coconut and ginger. Spoon into prepared muffin cups. Bake in preheated oven 20 to 25 minutes or until golden brown. In a small bowl, combine 1/4 cup sugar and nutmeg. Unmold hot puffs and immediately roll in melted butter, then in sugar mixture. Serve hot or cold. Makes 6 large or 18 miniature muffins.

Pumpkin-Pecan Bread

Inside and outside, it's a beautiful golden-brown color, thanks to pumpkin and all the flavorful spices.

1/2 cup butter or margarine, room temperature
1 cup sugar
2 eggs
1 cup canned pumpkin
1 teaspoon baking soda
1/2 teaspoon baking powder

1/2 teaspoon ground cinnamon
1/4 teaspoon ground cloves
1/2 teaspoon ground nutmeg
1/4 teaspoon grated orange peel
1-1/2 cups all-purpose flour
1/2 cup chopped pecans

Preheat oven to 350F (175C). Grease a 9" x 5" loaf pan. In a large bowl, cream butter and sugar. Beat in eggs and pumpkin. Add baking soda, baking powder, cinnamon, cloves, nutmeg, orange peel and flour; stir until smooth. Stir in pecans. Spoon into prepared pan. Bake in preheated oven 50 to 60 minutes or until a wooden pick inserted in center comes out clean. Remove from oven. Loosen sides of loaf from pan; turn out on a cooling rack. Slice when completely cool. Serve plain or with butter or cream cheese. Makes 1 loaf.

Blueberry-Sour-Cream Ring

For a more festive ring, substitute a powdered-sugar glaze for the powdered-sugar topping.

1 egg
3/4 cup granulated sugar
2 tablespoons butter or margarine, room temperature
1-1/2 cups all-purpose flour
1 teaspoon baking powder
1/2 teaspoon baking soda

1/4 teaspoon salt
1/4 teaspoon ground nutmeg
1/2 cup dairy sour cream
1/2 teaspoon vanilla extract
1 cup fresh or frozen blueberries
Powdered sugar

Preheat oven to 400F (205C). Grease an 8- or 9-inch ring mold. In a large bowl, beat egg, granulated sugar and butter until fluffy. In a medium bowl, combine flour, baking powder, baking soda, salt and nutmeg. Add flour mixture to egg mixture alternately with sour cream until well blended. Stir in vanilla. Fold in blueberries. Spoon into prepared ring mold. Bake in preheated oven 20 minutes or until top springs back when touched with your finger tip. Remove from oven. Cool on a rack 5 minutes. Loosen from sides; invert onto a cooling rack. Sprinkle with powdered sugar. Cut into thick slices. Serve warm or at room temperature. Makes 1 (8- or 9-inch) ring.

Apricot-Cheesecake Muffins

Although paper muffin-cup liners are handy for some muffins, this recipe works better if cups are greased rather than lined.

1/2 cup finely chopped dried apricots
2 tablespoons orange liqueur
2 tablespoons butter or margarine, room temperature
1 (3-oz.) package cream cheese, room temperature
1/4 cup sugar

1 egg
1 cup milk
2 teaspoons baking powder
1/4 teaspoon baking soda
1/4 teaspoon salt
2 cups all-purpose flour
1/2 teaspoon grated lemon peel

Preheat oven to 400F (205C). Grease 12 (2-1/2- to 3-inch) muffin cups. In a small bowl, combine apricots and liqueur; set aside. In a large bowl, cream butter, cream cheese and sugar. Beat in egg and milk. Stir in baking powder, baking soda, salt, flour and lemon peel. Add liqueur-soaked apricots and any remaining liqueur in bowl. Spoon batter into prepared muffin cups. Bake in preheated oven 20 to 22 minutes or until edges begin to brown. Remove from oven. Loosen from sides; invert immediately on a cooling rack. Makes 12 muffins.

Topsy-Turvy Maple-Walnut Pumpkin Muffins

*All the wonderful aromatic spices we associate with pumpkin pie,
plus a yummy sticky topping.*

12 walnut halves

2 tablespoons brown sugar

2 tablespoons butter or margarine, melted

1 tablespoon maple syrup

1 cup all-bran cereal

1 cup buttermilk

1 egg, beaten slightly

1 cup all-purpose flour

1/4 cup lightly packed brown sugar

2 teaspoons baking powder

1/2 teaspoon baking soda

1/4 teaspoon salt

1/2 teaspoon ground cinnamon

1/8 teaspoon ground ginger

1/4 teaspoon ground nutmeg

2 tablespoons vegetable oil

1/2 cup canned pumpkin

Preheat oven to 400F (205C). Place 1 walnut half in bottom of each of 12 (2-1/2- to 3-inch) muffin cups. In a small bowl, combine 2 tablespoons brown sugar, melted butter and maple syrup. Spoon mixture over each walnut half. In a large bowl, combine all-bran cereal and buttermilk. Stir in egg, flour, 1/4 cup brown sugar, baking powder, baking soda, salt, cinnamon, ginger, nutmeg, oil and pumpkin. Spoon batter over glazed nuts in muffin cups. Bake in preheated oven about 20 minutes or until top springs back when lightly touched with your finger tip. Remove from oven. Loosen from sides; invert immediately on a cooling rack. Serve warm or cool. Makes 12 muffins.

Molasses Corn Bread

Serve it plain, or spread with butter.

1 cup yellow cornmeal

1 cup all-purpose flour

1/2 cup whole-wheat flour

1 teaspoon baking soda

1 teaspoon baking powder

1/2 teaspoon salt

1/2 cup raisins, coarsely chopped

2 eggs, beaten slightly

3/4 cup buttermilk

1/2 cup molasses

3 tablespoons vegetable oil

Preheat oven to 325F (165C). Grease a 9-inch ring mold. In a large bowl, combine cornmeal, all-purpose flour, whole-wheat flour, baking soda, baking powder and salt; stir in raisins. In a small bowl, combine eggs, buttermilk, molasses and oil; add to flour mixture, stirring until blended. Spoon into prepared ring mold. Bake in preheated oven 27 to 30 minutes or until a wooden pick inserted in center comes out clean. Remove from oven. Cool in pan 10 minutes. Invert on a cooling rack. Serve warm or cool. Makes 1 (9-inch) ring.

Pizza Rolls

All the popular ingredients of a pizza contained in muffin cups.
Chewy, pizza-like texture with built-in tomato flavor.

1 (1/4-oz.) package active dry yeast (about 1 tablespoon)
1 teaspoon sugar
1/2 cup warm water (110F/45C)
1 teaspoon salt
3 tablespoons olive oil or vegetable oil
1 (6-oz.) can tomato paste
2 tablespoons chopped fresh basil

1 teaspoon dried leaf thyme, crushed
1/2 teaspoon dried leaf oregano, crushed
1/2 teaspoon fennel seeds, crushed
2-1/3 to 2-1/2 cups all-purpose flour
4 ounces mozzarella cheese, cut into 12 equal cubes
1 (2-oz.) can anchovy fillets, drained, optional
1/4 cup (3/4 oz.) grated Parmesan cheese

In a large bowl, dissolve yeast and sugar in warm water. Let stand about 5 minutes. Stir in salt, 2 tablespoons oil, tomato paste, basil, thyme, oregano, fennel and 1 cup flour. Beat 2 minutes or until well blended. Stir in 1-1/3 cups flour or enough to make a soft dough. Turn out dough on a lightly floured board. Knead about 1 minute, working in enough flour to make a stiff dough. Clean and grease bowl. Place dough in greased bowl, turning to grease all sides. Cover and let rise in a warm place until doubled in bulk, about 1 hour. Preheat oven to 375F (190C). Grease 12 (2-1/2- to 3-inch) muffin cups. Punch down dough; divide into 12 equal portions. Shape each portion into a ball; place in a prepared muffin cup. Press a cube of cheese firmly into center of each. Brush tops with remaining 1 tablespoon oil. Place 1/2 an anchovy fillet over top of each cheese cube, if desired. Sprinkle each with 1 teaspoon Parmesan cheese. Bake in preheated oven 18 minutes or until golden brown. Remove from oven. Loosen from sides; remove and place on a cooling rack. Serve warm. Makes 12 muffins.

Egg-Muffin Crowns

The secret of success is to use a good, thick Roquefort dressing and paper-thin turkey. If you use thicker turkey slices, you'll need only one for each muffin half.

3 English muffins, split
1 cup (4 oz.) shredded Monterey Jack cheese
2 tablespoons refrigerated thick Roquefort-cheese dressing or thick blue-cheese dressing

1 teaspoon chopped chives
1 (2.5-oz.) package thinly sliced smoked turkey (12 slices)
3 hard-cooked eggs, halved lengthwise
Paprika

Arrange muffin halves on a baking sheet. In a small bowl, combine Monterey Jack cheese, Roquefort dressing and chives. Arrange 2 slices turkey on each muffin half. Place 1 hard-cooked egg half, cut-side down, on turkey on each muffin half. Spoon 2 tablespoons cheese mixture over each. Broil 4 to 5 inches from heat source 3 minutes or until bubbly. Sprinkle with paprika. Serve immediately. Makes 6 muffin halves.

Eggs in a Bun

Our family frequently makes this recipe because it's so versatile.

6 hard-cooked eggs, chopped
1 (2.5-oz.) package thinly sliced smoked cooked beef, chopped
2 teaspoons Dijon-style mustard
2 teaspoons prepared horseradish

1/2 cup mayonnaise
1 tablespoon sweet-pickle relish
1/8 teaspoon pepper
6 (4-inch) French rolls

In a medium bowl, combine hard-cooked eggs, beef, mustard, horseradish, mayonnaise, relish and pepper; set aside. Scoop out center of each roll, leaving about 1/2 inch around sides and bottom. Use scooped out crumbs for another purpose. Fill rolls with egg mixture. Makes 6 servings.

Smoky Canoes

*Children love the idea of eating a canoe. If you have frankfurters
on hand, substitute them for sausages.*

1 tablespoon prepared mustard	1 (8-oz.) package refrigerator crescent rolls
1 teaspoon prepared horseradish	1 (12-oz.) package smoked sausage links (eight
2 tablespoons plum jam or preserves	4-1/2-inch links)

Preheat oven to 400F (205C). In a small bowl, combine mustard, horseradish and jam; set aside. Unroll crescent-roll dough. Divide dough into 4 rectangles with 2 triangles in each. With fingers, press out perforations. On a lightly floured board, roll out each rectangle to a 6-1/2-inch square. Cut each square in half to form 2 (6-1/2" x 3-1/4") rectangles. Spoon about 1 teaspoon mustard mixture lengthwise down center of each rectangle. Top each with a sausage link. Pinch dough over ends of sausage; fold dough up on sides of sausage to resemble a canoe. Place on a baking sheet. Repeat with remaining ingredients. Bake in preheated oven 10 minutes or until bread is golden. Serve warm. Makes 8 servings.

Casual Lunches

This mid-day meal has a different meaning for each of us, depending on our way of life. It may range from a sandwich in a brown bag or a quick visit to a fast-food establishment, to an elaborate multi-course luncheon at an elegant home or restaurant. Keeping this in mind, we tried to introduce a number of finger foods that can be adapted for a variety of situations.

If you're short of time, select a sandwich-type recipe, such as Turkey & Pistachios on a Bagel or Open-Faced Mini-Reubens. You can pick up bagels or French rolls at the bakery or market. The toppings are quick and easy to assemble. Add fresh fruit or a salad and a beverage, and you have a fast lunch. An ethnic theme is a good choice for a slightly more complicated menu. Goat-Cheese & Salmon Dumplings, Chicken-Mushroom Spring Rolls and Curried Java Foldovers are exciting new variations of more traditional combinations usually associated with won-ton or spring-roll wrappers.

If children were choosing their favorite, we're sure that Crunchy Corn-Dogs on a Stick would be given the blue ribbon.

Barbecued Chicken & Corn Pizza

Here's an unusual pizza with a favorite flavor combination of corn-on-the-cob, chicken and barbecue sauce. These baby ears of corn fit just right on mini-pizzas. (Photo on previous pages.)

1 (1/4-oz.) package active dry yeast (about 1 tablespoon)
1 teaspoon sugar
1 cup warm water (110F/45C)
1 teaspoon salt
2 tablespoons vegetable oil
3 to 3-1/4 cups all-purpose flour
1-1/2 cups chopped cooked chicken

6 tablespoons bottled barbecue sauce
1 (8-3/4-oz.) can or 1 (8-oz.) package frozen baby ears of corn
1/3 cup chopped green bell pepper
1-1/4 cups (5 oz.) shredded Cheddar cheese
Black pepper, optional
Fresh herbs for garnish

In a large bowl, dissolve yeast and sugar in warm water. Let stand about 5 minutes. Stir in salt, oil and 1 cup flour. Beat 2 minutes or until well blended. Stir in 1-1/2 to 2 cups flour or enough additional flour to make a soft dough. Turn out dough on a lightly floured board. Knead about 1 minute, working in enough flour to make a stiff dough. Clean and grease bowl. Place dough in greased bowl, turning to grease all sides. Cover and let rise in a warm place until doubled in bulk, about 40 to 45 minutes. Preheat oven to 425F (220C). In a small bowl, combine chicken and barbecue sauce. Punch down dough; divide dough into 8 equal pieces. On baking sheets, shape each dough piece into a 5-inch circle with a shallow rim. Spread equal amounts of chicken and sauce on dough. Arrange corn on top. Sprinkle with green pepper and cheese. Season with black pepper, if desired. Bake in preheated oven 18 to 20 minutes. Garnish with fresh herbs. Serve warm. Makes 8 (5-inch) pizzas.

Mini-Tortilla Pizzas

Serve with additional salsa for those who like a more spicy treat.

6 (5-inch) corn tortillas
2 tablespoons vegetable oil
1/2 pound bulk pork sausage, cooked, crumbled, drained
1/2 cup sliced ripe olives

1/4 cup green-chili salsa
1 cup (4 oz.) shredded Monterey Jack cheese
Dairy sour cream, optional
Chopped cilantro, optional

Preheat oven to 400F (205C). Brush 1 side of each tortilla with oil. Arrange tortillas, oiled side up, in a single layer on a 15" x 10" jelly-roll pan. Bake in preheated oven 10 minutes or until crispy and light brown. Sprinkle each tortilla with sausage; top with olives and salsa. Sprinkle with cheese. Return to oven 5 minutes or until cheese is bubbly. Remove from oven; top with sour cream and cilantro, if desired. Serve warm. Makes 6 servings.

Open-Faced Brie & Leek Flatbread

*Similar to a pizza with a quick and easy crust. When cut into
larger servings, use it as a main dish for lunch.*

2 cups buttermilk baking mix
3/4 teaspoon dried dill weed
1/2 cup butter or margarine, room temperature
1/4 cup boiling water
2 tablespoons butter or margarine
4 medium leeks, washed, thinly sliced

1/4 teaspoon salt
1/8 teaspoon pepper
4 ounces Brie cheese, cut into cubes
1/4 cup pine nuts
Cherry tomatoes, quartered

Preheat oven to 425F (220C). In a small bowl, combine baking mix, dill weed and 1/2 cup butter. Pour in boiling water, stirring until well blended. Press dough into a 15" x 10" jelly-roll pan. Bake in preheated oven 10 minutes or until light-golden color. Remove from oven. Reduce oven temperature to 375F (190C). Meanwhile, in a large skillet, melt 2 tablespoons butter. Add leeks; cook over medium heat until limp. Stir in salt and pepper. Spoon leek mixture over baked crust. Top with Brie and pine nuts. Bake in preheated oven 3 minutes or until cheese begins to melt. Remove from oven. Cut in 1-1/2- to 1-3/4-inch pieces. Garnish with cherry-tomato pieces. Serve warm. Makes 40 to 50 small servings.

Pizza-Rice Roll-Ups

*Your favorite pizza ingredients combined with rice to form a tasty
finger food.*

1/2 cup uncooked long-grain white rice
1/4 cup (1 oz.) shredded mozzarella cheese
2 mushrooms, finely chopped
1 tablespoon butter or margarine, melted
1/4 teaspoon dried leaf oregano, crushed

1/8 teaspoon salt
1/16 teaspoon pepper
2 tablespoons grated Parmesan cheese
16 thin slices salami

Cook rice according to package directions; cool. Stir in mozzarella cheese, mushrooms, butter, oregano, salt, pepper and Parmesan cheese. Spoon about 2 tablespoons rice mixture along center of each slice of salami; roll up. Cover and refrigerate several hours, if desired. At serving time, preheat oven to 350F (175C). Warm roll-ups in a shallow baking pan 10 minutes or until hot. Serve immediately. Makes 16 roll-ups.

Barbecued Beef on a Bun

For additional crunch to this recipe, top barbecued beef with a thin layer of shredded cabbage or a slice of sweet onion.

2 pounds beef stewing pieces or beef chuck
   roast, cut in cubes
1 small onion, diced
1 cup ketchup
2 tablespoons brown sugar
1 teaspoon dry mustard

2 tablespoons Worcestershire sauce
1/2 cup beef stock or bouillon
1/4 teaspoon salt
1/8 teaspoon pepper
10 Kaiser rolls or onion rolls, split, warmed

In a 4-quart Dutch oven, combine meat with remaining ingredients except rolls. Cover and simmer over low heat 2-1/2 to 3 hours or until meat is very tender. Place warm meat mixture in a food processor fitted with the metal blade. Processly briefly to shred. Spoon about 1/2 cup meat and sauce onto each roll. Serve hot. Makes 10 servings.

Crunchy Corn-Dogs on a Stick

All kinds of mustard are good for dipping. We enjoy sweet and spicy or the favorite all-American yellow variety.

1 cup all-purpose flour
1/2 cup cornmeal
1 tablespoon sugar
1-1/2 teaspoons baking powder
1/4 teaspoon salt
2 tablespoons vegetable shortening

1 egg, beaten slightly
3/4 cup milk
Oil for deep-frying
8 frankfurters
Mustard, if desired

In a shallow, medium bowl, combine flour, cornmeal, sugar, baking powder and salt. With a pastry blender or fork, cut vegetable shortening into flour mixture until mixture resembles fine crumbs. Add egg and milk; blend well. Pour vegetable oil to a 2-inch depth in a deep-fryer or large saucepan. Heat oil to 375F (190C) or until a 1-inch bread cube turns golden brown in 50 seconds. Pat frankfurters dry with paper towels. Insert a wooden skewer into 1 end of each frankfurter. Dip each frankfurter into batter, spreading evenly and coating all sides. Cook 2 coated frankfurters at a time in hot oil until golden brown. Drain on paper towels. Serve warm with mustard, if desired. Makes 8 servings.

Open-Faced Mini-Reubens

A classic sandwich combination that's spicy enough to be appealing. Make on small rolls for ease in handling.

4 small round French rolls, split
2 tablespoons butter or margarine, room temperature
8 slices Swiss cheese, halved
1 cup sauerkraut, well drained

2 teaspoons prepared mustard
16 thin slices cooked corned beef or pastrami
1/4 cup mayonnaise
1 tablespoon chili sauce

Lightly spread cut sides of rolls with butter. Arrange half the Swiss cheese on rolls. Top with sauerkraut, mustard and corned beef or pastrami. In a small bowl, combine mayonnaise and chili sauce; spoon over meat. Top with remaining Swiss cheese. Place open-faced sandwiches on a broiler pan. Broil 5 to 6 inches from heat source 2 to 3 minutes or until cheese melts. Remove from broiler; serve warm. Makes 8 small open-faced sandwiches.

Layered Tuna-Egg Loaf

A hearty three-layer sandwich that can be used as a main dish.

1 (20-inch) French bread baguette
4 hard-cooked eggs, chopped
1/4 cup chopped ripe olives
2 tablespoons canned diced green chilies
1/2 cup (2 oz.) shredded Cheddar cheese

1 (6-1/2-oz.) can tuna, drained, flaked
1/4 cup mayonnaise
2 tablespoons finely chopped green onion
2 tablespoons chopped red bell pepper

Preheat oven to 375F (190C). Slice bread lengthwise into 3 equal pieces. In a small bowl, combine eggs, olives, chilies and cheese. Spread mixture on cut side of bottom layer of bread. Top with second bread layer. In a small bowl, combine tuna, mayonnaise, green onion and red pepper. Spread on middle layer of bread. Cover with top of bread. Wrap entire loaf in foil. Bake in preheated oven 20 minutes or until hot. Remove from oven; cut loaf crosswise into 2- or 2-1/2-inch slices. Serve warm. Makes 8 to 10 servings.

Mustard-Chicken Rolls

*Leave each roll-up whole for a traditional-size serving or cut each
into three or four pieces for appetizer servings.*

4 boneless chicken-breast halves, skinned (about
   1 lb.)
8 small green onions
Salt
Pepper

1/4 cup butter or margarine, melted
2 teaspoons sweet and spicy mustard
1 teaspoon Worcestershire sauce
1 cup soft bread crumbs

Preheat oven to 350F (175C). Lightly pound chicken breasts between waxed paper until they are about 1/4 inch thick. Cut each chicken breast in half lengthwise. Place 1 green onion lengthwise on each chicken piece. Sprinkle with salt and pepper. Roll each chicken piece, securing with a small wooden pick, if necessary. In a small shallow bowl, combine melted butter, mustard and Worcestershire sauce. Dip each chicken roll in butter mixture, then roll in bread crumbs. Place in a shallow baking pan. Bake in preheated oven 17 to 20 minutes or until juices run clear when pierced with a fork. Serve hot. Makes 8 servings.

Spinach-Filled Filo Cups

*We prefer to eat them while they're hot from the oven, but they're
still good at room temperature.*

1 (10-oz.) package frozen chopped spinach,
   thawed
10 medium mushrooms, chopped
3/4 cup (6 oz.) ricotta cheese
3 tablespoons pine nuts, chopped
1/8 teaspoon ground nutmeg

1 egg, beaten slightly
1/2 teaspoon seasoned salt
1/4 cup (3/4 oz.) grated Parmesan cheese
4 sheets filo dough
6 tablespoons butter or margarine, melted

Preheat oven to 375F (190C). Drain spinach in a strainer, using the back of a spoon to press out excess liquid. In a medium bowl, combine drained spinach, mushrooms, ricotta cheese, pine nuts, nutmeg, egg, seasoned salt and 2 tablespoons Parmesan cheese; set aside. Brush each sheet of filo with melted butter; stack filo sheets. Cut filo in fourths crosswise and thirds lengthwise to form 12 (4-layer) squares. Gently press each square into a (2-1/2- to 3-inch) muffin cup or a 6-ounce custard cup. Spoon 1/4 cup spinach mixture into each filo-lined cup. Sprinkle with remaining 2 tablespoons Parmesan cheese. Bake in preheated oven 25 minutes or until golden brown and filling is set. Remove from oven; let stand 5 minutes. Remove from cups. Makes 12 servings.

Roquefort Tortas

*Create an impressive luncheon plate with one of these tortas
encircled by thin red apple slices, juicy orange segments and a
cluster of green seedless grapes.*

2/3 cup zwieback crumbs (7 or 8 slices)
2 tablespoons toasted sesame seeds
3 tablespoons butter or margarine, melted
1 (3-oz.) package cream cheese, room
    temperature
2 ounces Roquefort or blue cheese, crumbled

1 egg
1/4 cup dairy sour cream
1/4 teaspoon grated onion
1/2 teaspoon Worcestershire sauce

In a small bowl, combine zwieback crumbs, sesame seeds and butter. Press mixture onto bottoms and sides of 4 (6-ounce) custard cups; refrigerate. Preheat oven to 350F (175C). In a medium bowl, beat cream cheese and Roquefort cheese until well blended. Beat in egg, sour cream, onion and Worcestershire sauce. Spoon into crumb-lined cups. Bake in preheated oven 25 minutes. Turn off heat and leave in oven with door ajar 30 minutes. Refrigerate overnight or several hours until thoroughly chilled. To remove from pan, loosen with a small knife. Makes 4 servings.

Chili-Cheese Boats

*A hearty, satisfying and flavorful main dish that's easy to pick up
and eat on the run. Also, an unusual presentation for homemade
chili.*

1 (15-oz.) can chili with beans
1 (2-1/4-oz.) can sliced ripe olives, drained
1/3 cup diced onion
3 tablespoons canned diced green chilies

1 cup (4 oz.) shredded Cheddar cheese
12 (3-inch) sourdough French rolls
2 tablespoons chopped green onion for garnish

Preheat oven to 400F (205C). In a medium bowl, combine chili with beans, olives, onion, green chilies and 1/2 cup cheese. Scoop out center of each roll, leaving about 1/2 inch around sides and bottom. Use scooped out crumbs for another purpose. Spoon about 3 tablespoons chili mixture into each roll. Arrange on a baking sheet; bake in preheated oven 12 minutes or until rolls are crisp on outside and filling is hot. Immediately sprinkle top of each roll with remaining cheese. Garnish with green onion. Serve warm. Makes 12 servings.

Mandarin Stir-Fry in Pita Bread

*After you slice off the top of a pita bread, insert that piece in the
bottom of the pocket to be filled.*

2 tablespoons vegetable oil

2 teaspoons sesame oil

1-1/3 cups small uncooked shrimp, shelled, halved

24 Chinese pea pods, halved

1/4 cup sliced green onions

1/2 cup sliced water chestnuts

1-1/2 tablespoons soy sauce

1 teaspoon grated fresh ginger

4 (6-inch) pita bread rounds, warmed

Fresh herbs, optional

In a small skillet, heat vegetable oil and sesame oil. Add shrimp; sauté about 1 minute. Stir in pea pods, green onions, water chestnuts, soy sauce and ginger; cook 1 minute. Slice off top of each pita round. Place top inside bottom to reinforce it. Spoon shrimp mixture into warm pita rounds. Garnish with fresh herbs, if desired. Serve warm. Makes 4 servings.

Chicken-Mushroom Spring Rolls

*While filling spring rolls, cover opened package of spring-roll
wrappers with a damp towel to prevent drying out.*

2 boneless chicken-breast halves, skinned (about 1/2 lb.)

6 medium mushrooms, quartered

1 green onion, chopped

1 tablespoon chopped fresh parsley

1 teaspoon chopped fresh tarragon

1/2 teaspoon salt

1/8 teaspoon pepper

2 tablespoons vegetable oil

8 spring-roll wrappers

2 tablespoons butter or margarine, melted

Preheat oven to 400F (205C). Cut chicken into small pieces. In a blender or food processor fitted with the metal blade, combine chicken, mushrooms, green onion, parsley, tarragon, salt and pepper. Process until very finely chopped, but not pureed. In a medium skillet, heat oil. Add chicken mixture; cook 3 to 4 minutes or until chicken is done. Spoon about 1/4 cup chicken mixture diagonally across a spring-roll wrapper. Fold bottom corner over filling, then fold 2 side corners toward center; roll toward top corner. Place roll, seam-side down, on a baking sheet. Repeat with remaining ingredients. Brush rolls with melted butter. Bake in preheated oven 15 minutes or until golden brown. Drain on paper towels. Serve warm. Makes 8 servings.

Italian Envelopes

A Chinese won-ton wrapper around Italian ingredients results in good American eating.

1 egg, beaten slightly
1/2 cup (4 oz.) ricotta cheese
1/2 cup (2 oz.) finely chopped salami
1/2 cup (2 oz.) finely chopped mozzarella cheese
1/4 teaspoon dried leaf oregano, crushed

1/4 teaspoon salt
1/8 teaspoon pepper
18 to 20 square won-ton wrappers
1/4 cup vegetable oil
2 tablespoons grated Parmesan cheese

In a small bowl, combine egg, ricotta cheese, salami, mozzarella cheese, oregano, salt and pepper. Place a won-ton wrapper at an angle with 1 corner facing you. Spoon about 1 tablespoon cheese mixture in center of wrapper. Lightly brush edges with water. Fold right and left corners inward, overlapping slightly. Then bring bottom and top corners together, overlapping slightly in middle. Repeat until all ingredients are used. Heat oil in a large skillet. Fry a single layer of envelopes at a time, until golden on both sides. Remove from skillet; immediately sprinkle tops with Parmesan cheese. Drain on paper towels. Repeat until all are cooked. Serve warm. Makes 18 to 20 servings.

Artichoke-Pita Puffs

Use a California green chili or jalapeño pepper, depending on your tolerance of hot foods.

1 (6-oz.) jar marinated artichoke hearts, drained, finely chopped
1/2 cup (1.5 oz.) grated Parmesan cheese
1/2 cup mayonnaise
2 tablespoons finely chopped green chili or jalapeño pepper

1 teaspoon lime juice
1/2 teaspoon grated onion
2 (6-inch) pita bread rounds

In a small bowl, combine chopped artichoke hearts, cheese, mayonnaise, green chili, lime juice and onion. Split each pita bread round into 2 thin circles. Spread artichoke mixture on cut sides of each pita round. Arrange pitas on a baking sheet. Broil 4 to 5 inches from heat source until bubbly and golden. Remove from broiler; serve immediately. Makes 4 large servings or cut each pita round into 5 or 6 wedges.

Curried Java Foldovers

Tempting morsels with spicy flavors from Southeast Asia.

3 tablespoons vegetable oil
1/2 pound lean ground pork
1 garlic clove, crushed
1 teaspoon curry powder
1 teaspoon grated fresh ginger
2 tablespoons flaked coconut

1 tablespoon chutney, fruit pieces finely chopped
1/4 teaspoon salt
1/8 teaspoon pepper
2 tablespoons plain yogurt
22 (3-inch) round won-ton wrappers

In a medium skillet, heat 1 tablespoon oil. Add pork and garlic, cooking until pork is no longer pink; drain thoroughly. In a medium bowl, combine drained pork, curry powder, ginger, coconut, chutney, salt and pepper; stir in yogurt. Spoon about 1 tablespoon filling in lower half of a won-ton wrapper. Lightly brush edge of wrapper with water. Fold wrapper over to form a half-moon shape. Press with a fork to seal, if desired. Repeat with remaining filling and won-ton wrappers. Heat remaining 2 tablespoons oil in a large skillet. Cook half the foldovers until golden on both sides. Repeat with remaining foldovers. Serve warm. Makes 22 foldovers.

Goat-Cheese & Salmon Dumplings

Some markets do not have round won-ton wrappers. If you have this problem, buy square ones and trim the corners to make a round shape.

2 eggs, beaten slightly
1-3/4 cups (7 oz.) crumbled goat cheese
1/2 cup half and half
1 tablespoon finely chopped fresh basil
1 teaspoon finely chopped chives

1/4 teaspoon salt
1/8 teaspoon pepper
2 ounces smoked salmon (lox), chopped
24 (3-inch) round won-ton wrappers

Preheat oven to 350F (175C). Lightly grease 24 miniature muffin cups. In a medium bowl, combine eggs, cheese, half and half, basil, chives, salt and pepper; stir in salmon. Place a won-ton wrapper in each greased muffin cup. Spoon about 1 tablespoon cheese mixture into each cup. Bake in preheated oven 15 minutes or until filling is firm. Remove from oven; serve warm. Makes 24 servings.

Confetti Ham Roll-Ups

An interesting roll-up that's really a combination salad and main dish you can eat on the run.

1 cup (4 oz.) shredded Monterey Jack cheese

1 medium carrot, peeled, grated

1 tablespoon dairy sour cream

1/2 teaspoon grated orange peel

1 teaspoon finely chopped chives

1/2 teaspoon grated fresh ginger

1 (12-oz.) package boiled ham (10 four-inch slices)

20 orange segments, about 2 large oranges

In a small bowl, combine cheese, carrot, sour cream, orange peel, chives and ginger. Spread about 1 tablespoon mixture on each slice of ham. Arrange 2 orange segments on each; then roll up. Refrigerate, seam-side down, at least 2 hours. Serve whole or cut each roll-up in half. Makes 10 large or 20 small roll-ups.

Acapulco Puffs

Substitute jalapeño peppers for chilies if you enjoy a hotter dish.

1-1/2 cups (6 oz.) shredded Cheddar cheese

1/3 cup mayonnaise

1 egg, beaten slightly

1 tablespoon finely chopped green onion

2 tablespoons canned diced green chilies

1/2 teaspoon Dijon-style mustard

1/2 teaspoon Worcestershire sauce

4 slices bacon, cooked, crumbled

1 large tomato, cut into 8 thin slices

4 sourdough English muffins, split, toasted

1 avocado, cut into 8 thin slices

Preheat oven to 350F (175C). In a small bowl, combine cheese, mayonnaise, egg, green onion, chilies, mustard, Worcestershire sauce and bacon. Place a tomato slice on each muffin half. Top each with about 2-1/2 tablespoons cheese mixture. Place on a baking sheet. Bake in preheated oven 10 to 15 minutes or until golden and puffy. Remove from oven. Top each with a slice of avocado. Serve warm. Makes 8 servings.

Rhinecastle Roll-Ups

*Mustard dressing is not absolutely necessary with the roll-ups, but
it does lend a zesty accent to the dish.*

8 ounces liverwurst

1/4 cup mayonnaise

1 tablespoon sweet-pickle relish

1 small head Boston lettuce

In a small bowl, combine liverwurst, mayonnaise and relish; blend well. Separate lettuce into individual leaves; spread liverwurst mixture on each leaf. Fold ends in and roll up; secure with a wooden pick, if necessary. Serve with Mustard Dressing for dipping. Makes 10 to 12 roll-ups.

Mustard Dressing:

3 tablespoons Dijon-style mustard

3 tablespoons red-wine vinegar

1/2 teaspoon seasoned salt

1/4 teaspoon seasoned pepper

1/4 teaspoon fines herbs

3/4 cup vegetable oil

In a blender or food processor fitted with the metal blade, combine mustard, vinegar, seasoned salt, seasoned pepper and fines herbs. With motor running, pour in oil very slowly. Mixture will become about the consistency of mayonnaise. Makes about 1 cup dressing.

Romana Blintzes

*A wonderful combination of flavors and cultures that appeals to
the American melting pot of tastes.*

1/2 cup (4 oz.) ricotta cheese

1 egg, beaten slightly

1 ounce pepperoni, chopped

2 tablespoons chopped green onion

3 medium mushrooms, chopped

1/4 teaspoon salt

1/8 teaspoon pepper

4 (8-inch) flour tortillas

2 tablespoons grated Parmesan cheese

2 teaspoons butter or margarine, melted

Preheat oven to 375F (190C). In a small bowl, combine ricotta cheese, egg, pepperoni, green onion, mushrooms, salt and pepper. Spoon about 1/4 cup mixture in center of each tortilla; sprinkle each with Parmesan cheese. Fold both sides of each tortilla over filling; then fold top and bottom to slightly overlap in center. Brush with melted butter. Place filled tortillas, folded-side down, in a shallow baking pan. Bake, uncovered, in preheated oven 12 to 15 minutes. Serve hot. Makes 4 servings.

Tortilla-Cheese Stack

*If you're in a hurry at serving time, brown the individual tortillas
ahead of time; then put it together in a few minutes.*

1/2 cup vegetable oil
6 (8-inch) flour tortillas
1 (8-1/4-oz.) can refried beans
2 green onions, chopped

1 medium tomato, chopped
1 (4-oz.) can diced green chilies
1/2 cup (2 oz.) shredded Monterey Jack cheese
1/2 cup (2 oz.) shredded Cheddar cheese

Heat oil in a 9-inch skillet. Cook both sides of each tortilla in hot oil until crispy and a light-golden color; drain on paper towels. Preheat oven to 350F (175C). Place 2 cooked tortillas on a large baking sheet. Spread each with half the refried beans; sprinkle each with green onion. Top each with a second tortilla. Sprinkle each with half the tomatoes and chilies; then with Monterey Jack cheese. Top each with a third tortilla; sprinkle each with Cheddar cheese. Bake in preheated oven 5 to 8 minutes or until cheese melts. Remove from oven. Cut each stack into 5 or 6 wedges. Serve immediately. Makes 10 to 12 servings.

Bean-Tortilla Crisp

*Pick them up and eat them like a taco. Spoon on a bit of your
favorite hot sauce or salsa for additional spice.*

2 slices bacon, diced
1 (15-oz.) can pinto beans
3/4 teaspoon ground cumin
1 jalapeño pepper, finely chopped (about 1-1/2
    tablespoons)
1/4 cup chopped onion

1 large garlic clove, finely chopped
10 (5-inch) flour tortillas
1 cup (4 oz.) crumbled goat cheese
1/2 cup chopped red onion
3 to 4 tablespoons vegetable oil

In a medium skillet, cook bacon until slightly crisp. Drain beans, reserving 1/4 cup liquid. Partially mash beans; then add to cooked bacon. Stir in cumin, jalapeño pepper, onion and garlic. Simmer 2 to 3 minutes. If mixture is too dry, add some of the reserved bean liquid. Spread about 2 tablespoons bean mixture on half of each tortilla. Top each with 1 generous tablespoon goat cheese and 2 teaspoons red onion. Fold each in a half-moon shape. Heat 2 tablespoons oil in a large skillet or griddle. Cook 3 or 4 filled tortillas on both sides until golden. Repeat, adding additional oil as necessary, until all filled tortillas are cooked. Serve warm. Makes 10 servings.

Shrimp-Stuffed Artichokes

There's a bit of shrimp mixture to eat with each leaf. When you get to the center, discard the fuzzy choke. Dip each artichoke heart in the wine left in the bottom of the pan.

1-1/2 cups garlic-flavored croutons
1/2 pound cooked, shelled small shrimp
1/4 cup loosely packed watercress leaves
10 medium mushrooms
1/4 cup butter or margarine

1/4 teaspoon salt
1/8 teaspoon pepper
1 egg
4 medium artichokes
1 cup dry white wine

In a blender or food processor fitted with the metal blade, combine croutons, shrimp, watercress, mushrooms, butter, salt, pepper and egg. Blend until finely chopped, but not pureed; set aside. Slice about 1 inch off top of each artichoke. With scissors, trim about 1/2 inch off each leaf tip. Cook artichokes in a saucepan of boiling water 25 to 35 minutes or until barely tender. Turn cooked artichokes upside down on paper towels to drain. Gently pull leaves away from center of artichoke, being careful not to break them off. Starting at the bottom of the artichoke, place a small amount of shrimp stuffing into each leaf pocket. Preheat oven to 350F (175C). Place stuffed artichokes in a 13" x 9" baking pan. Pour wine around, but not on, stuffed artichokes. Lightly cover with foil. Bake in preheated oven 20 minutes; basting artichokes with wine twice during baking. Serve warm. To eat, pull out individual leaves with stuffing. Makes 4 servings.

Walk-Away Italian Salad

The diameter of mortadella or salami determines the number of servings. If possible, purchase large thin slices of meat that can be neatly wrapped around the filling.

1/2 cup orzo pasta
1 medium zucchini, chopped
1 medium tomato, chopped
1/2 cup (2 oz.) diced mozzarella cheese
2 tablespoons olive oil or vegetable oil
2 tablespoons tarragon vinegar

1 tablespoon finely chopped fresh parsley
1 garlic clove, crushed
1/2 teaspoon dry mustard
1/2 teaspoon salt
1/8 teaspoon pepper
Large thin slices of mortadella or salami

Cook pasta as package directs until tender; drain. In a medium bowl, combine cooked pasta, zucchini, tomato and cheese. In a small bowl, combine oil, vinegar, parsley, garlic, mustard, salt and pepper. Pour oil mixture over vegetables; toss to coat well. Cover and refrigerate at least 2 hours. Place 3 to 4 tablespoons vegetable mixture in center of each large slice of meat. Roll up, securing with a wooden pick if necessary. Makes 12 to 16 salad roll-ups.

Tip
Orzo is a very small oval-shaped pasta about the size and color of rice. It should be cooked in boiling water until tender, but still keeping its shape.

◆

Picante-Stuffed Pita

Spicy but nice! For less heat, substitute a milder sauce.

2 cups finely chopped cooked chicken or turkey
1 avocado, finely chopped
1 cup finely chopped lettuce
1 California green chili or jalapeño pepper, finely chopped

1/4 teaspoon salt
3 (6-inch) pita bread rounds, halved crosswise
3/4 cup picante sauce or salsa
2 tablespoons dairy sour cream

In a medium bowl, combine chicken, avocado, lettuce, green chili and salt. Spoon mixture into each half pita bread; top with picante sauce and a dollop of sour cream. Serve immediately. Makes 6 servings.

Taste-of-Athens Rice Cakes

*Just the right combination of ingredients for rice cakes with a
Greek accent.*

4 ounces feta cheese
2 tablespoons plain yogurt
1/4 cup chopped ripe olives
2 tablespoons chopped red bell pepper

Dash hot-pepper sauce
8 rice cakes
1 tablespoon sliced green onion

In a small bowl, combine feta cheese, yogurt, olives, red bell pepper and hot-pepper sauce. Spread cheese mixture on rice cakes. Sprinkle each with green onion. Serve immediately. Makes 8 servings.

Turkey & Pistachios on a Bagel

Hearty and filling for family fare, yet impressive for special guests.

2 cups diced cooked turkey or chicken
1/4 cup dairy sour cream
1/4 cup mayonnaise
1 teaspoon chopped fresh tarragon
1/4 teaspoon salt

1/8 teaspoon pepper
1/4 cup pistachios
4 bagels, split, toasted
1/4 cup jellied cranberry sauce, cut into cubes

In a blender or food processor fitted with the metal blade, combine turkey, sour cream, mayonnaise, tarragon, salt, pepper and pistachios. Process until finely chopped. Spread turkey mixture on cut sides of toasted bagels. Top with small cubes of cranberry sauce. Makes 8 servings.

Crab 'n' Avocado Filled Croissant

*Increase or decrease the picante sauce, depending on your
tolerance of hot spicy food.*

1 medium avocado, peeled, mashed
1 tablespoon minced green onion
2 tablespoons plain yogurt
1/2 teaspoon Worcestershire sauce
1/4 teaspoon salt
1 tablespoon picante sauce

8 ounces fresh, frozen or canned crabmeat,
 drained, flaked
4 croissants, split
2 medium tomatoes, sliced
Lettuce

In medium bowl, combine mashed avocado, green onion, yogurt, Worcestershire sauce, salt, picante sauce and crab meat. Spread crab mixture on cut side of bottom half of croissant. Top with tomato slices; then lettuce. Cover with top half of croissant; cut in half, crosswise. Makes 4 sandwiches.

Pickup Dinners

Today, there is less emphasis on a set time and type of food for each meal. We may eat foods associated with breakfast at dinner time and vice versa. Small portions of several different foods are replacing the traditional "meat and potatoes" menu. People like to try bits and pieces with different flavors. Formerly, a restaurant would present a lunch menu two or three hours in the middle of the day. Then, after a certain hour in the afternoon, an entirely different menu was presented for dinner. Today, this restaurant is likely to have the same menu from noon until midnight.

These restaurant trends are spilling over into our homes. Busy families want to prepare and eat meals quickly, leaving time for leisure activities, school and work. In many families, individuals eat at different times throughout the day. For this reason, proportioned units of food are handy for picking up and eating quickly. That's why finger foods fit into today's way of life.

Remember that the main dish is the heart of the meal. Other foods radiate from it. For example, start a menu with Tasty Oriental Beef Bundles, then add a couple of your favorite vegetables or salads. If you're short on time, pick up part of the meal at a deli or take-out store. For easy finger foods, cut a colorful variety of seasonal fresh fruits or vegetables into small units. Arrange them on a tray; have small picks nearby, in case they're needed.

Pesto-Style Chicken Fajitas

Although chicken is our first choice for this recipe, we enjoy
substituting beef strips for a change of flavor.
(Photo on previous pages.)

1 cup lightly packed fresh basil leaves
1/4 cup lightly packed fresh parsley leaves
1 garlic clove, chopped
1 tablespoon olive oil
1/2 cup (4 oz.) ricotta cheese
2 tablespoons grated Parmesan cheese
2 boneless chicken-breast halves, skinned (about
   1/2 lb.)

1 tablespoon vegetable oil
1 cup sliced broccoli
1/2 cup sliced red bell pepper
1/2 cup sliced water chestnuts
1/4 teaspoon salt
1/8 teaspoon black pepper
4 (7-inch) flour tortillas, warmed
2 tablespoons pine nuts

In a blender or food processor fitted with the metal blade, combine basil, parsley, garlic, olive oil, ricotta cheese and Parmesan cheese. Process until chopped but not pureed; set aside. Cut chicken into thin strips. In a large skillet or wok, heat vegetable oil. Stir-fry chicken strips and broccoli in hot oil until chicken is done. Stir in red pepper, water chestnuts, salt and black pepper. Spoon onto warm tortillas; spoon pureed basil mixture over top. Sprinkle with pine nuts. Fold tortillas over. Serve warm. Makes 4 servings.

Munchy Sesame Wings

It takes 20 to 22 round sesame crackers to make enough crumbs
to coat chicken wings.

1 tablespoon soy sauce
1 garlic clove, crushed
1/3 cup Dijon-style mustard
2 tablespoons butter or margarine, melted
1/4 teaspoon salt
1/8 teaspoon pepper

1 cup sesame-cracker crumbs
1 teaspoon grated fresh ginger or 1/4 teaspoon
   ground ginger
20 chicken-wing drumettes or 10 chicken wings
   divided in half

Preheat oven to 350F (175C). In a small bowl, combine soy sauce, garlic, mustard, butter, salt and pepper. In a shallow bowl, combine cracker crumbs and ginger. Brush soy-sauce mixture on chicken wings. Roll sauce-coated wing pieces in crumbs to lightly coat. Place crumb-coated wing pieces in a single layer on a 15" x 10" jelly-roll pan. Bake in preheated oven 45 to 50 minutes or until golden brown. Cool in pan 5 minutes. Serve warm. Makes 20 wing pieces.

Chicken Siam

Baking results in a more moist dish; broiled chicken is more crunchy.

6 boneless chicken-breast halves, skinned (about 1-1/2 lbs.)
1 tablespoon butter or margarine, melted
1 tablespoon vegetable oil
1/2 cup salted peanuts

1/3 cup chutney
1 tablespoon lemon juice
1 jalapeño pepper, seeded, chopped
1/2 teaspoon salt
1/2 cup half and half

Preheat oven to 350F (175C). Cut chicken breasts lengthwise into 4 or 5 long strips; thread each strip on a 6-inch skewer. Arrange skewers in a large shallow baking pan. In a small bowl, combine butter and oil; brush on chicken. In a blender or food processor fitted with the metal blade, combine peanuts, chutney, lemon juice, jalapeño pepper, salt and half and half. Process until finely chopped, but not pureed. Brush top of chicken with peanut sauce. Bake in preheated oven 7 minutes. Turn kabobs. Brush other side with sauce. Return to oven; bake 3 minutes or until done. Serve warm. Makes 24 to 30 kabobs.

Variation
If you prefer broiled chicken, brush kabobs with sauce. Broil 4 to 5 inches from heat source 3 minutes. Turn kabobs; brush with sauce. Broil 2 minutes or until chicken is done.

Herbed Chicken Patties

Depending on your food processor, you may have to process the chicken in two batches and then combine it in a bowl.

1/2 cup cornflake crumbs
1 teaspoon paprika
3/4 teaspoon celery salt
1/2 teaspoon onion powder
1/4 teaspoon garlic powder
1/4 teaspoon ground sage
1/4 teaspoon ground thyme

1/8 teaspoon pepper
1 teaspoon vegetable oil
1-1/2 pounds skinless, boneless chicken thighs, cut into 1-inch pieces
1 egg white
1 tablespoon ice water
1 teaspoon chicken bouillon granules

In a small bowl, combine crumbs, paprika, celery salt, onion powder, garlic powder, sage, thyme, pepper and vegetable oil; blend well. Set crumb mixture aside. In a food processor fitted with the metal blade, combine chicken, egg white, ice water and bouillon granules. Process until finely ground and a paste forms. Preheat oven to 375F (190C). Grease a large baking sheet. Moisten your fingers with cold water; form chicken mixture into 1-1/2- to 1-3/4-inch patties. Dip each patty into crumb mixture, pressing crumbs in lightly with your finger tips. Place patties on prepared baking sheet. Bake in preheated oven 20 minutes, turning patties over after 10 minutes. Serve hot. Makes 30 to 35 patties.

Chicken-Leek Filo Fingers

When cleaning leeks, trim and discard tough, dark-green tops.
Use only white and light-green parts. Be sure to wash leeks well
to remove all sand and grit.

2 boneless chicken-breast halves, skinned, cut in
    small pieces (about 1/2 lb.)
1/4 pound prosciutto, chopped
2 tablespoons butter or margarine
1 small leek, cleaned, thinly sliced
2 tablespoons grated Parmesan cheese

2 tablespoons pine nuts, chopped
1/2 teaspoon finely chopped fresh tarragon leaves
1/8 teaspoon pepper
1 egg, beaten slightly
8 sheets filo dough
1/2 cup butter or margarine, melted

In a food processor fitted with the metal blade, combine chicken and prosciutto. Process until finely chopped, but not pureed. In a large skillet over medium heat, melt 2 tablespoons butter. Add leek; sauté until soft. Stir in chicken mixture; cook, stirring frequently, until chicken is done. Remove from heat. Stir in Parmesan cheese, pine nuts, tarragon, pepper and egg. Preheat oven to 400F (205C). Brush 1 sheet filo with melted butter; fold in half crosswise and then half again, resulting in 1/4 original size. Turn folded filo so long side faces you. Place 1/4 cup filling just below center of filo. Roll wrapper a half turn over so filling is covered. Fold in 2 sides to meet in middle. Roll up filo, ending with seam-side down. Brush with melted butter. Repeat with remaining filling and filo. Place filled rolls on a baking sheet. Bake in preheated oven 15 to 18 minutes or until golden. Serve hot. Makes 8 rolls.

Islandia Fish Kabobs

Use your favorite kind of steak fish. We enjoy using halibut,
swordfish or sea bass.

1-1/2 pounds fish steak
1/3 cup soy sauce
1 tablespoon lemon juice
2 tablespoons chopped green onion
1 tablespoon vegetable oil

1 tablespoon grated fresh ginger
1 tablespoon toasted sesame seeds
1 teaspoon sugar
1/8 teaspoon pepper

Cut fish into 1-1/2-inch squares. Using 4 or 5 (10-inch) skewers, arrange 3 or 4 fish cubes on each skewer. Place skewers in an 11" x 7" baking dish. In a blender or food processor fitted with the metal blade, combine remaining ingredients; process until well blended. Pour mixture over kabobs; cover and refrigerate at least 1 hour. Remove kabobs from marinade. Broil kabobs 4 to 5 inches from heat source 6 minutes. Turn kabobs; brush with marinade. Broil 3 minutes or until fish flakes easily with a fork. Serve hot. Makes 4 or 5 servings.

Favorite Butterflied Shrimp

Leave tails on shrimp for ease in picking up and dipping into your favorite sauce.

1 pound large uncooked shrimp (about 16)
Oil for deep-frying
1/3 cup all-purpose flour
1/4 teaspoon salt
1/8 teaspoon pepper

1/8 teaspoon seasoned salt
1 egg
1 tablespoon water
1/2 cup fine dry bread crumbs

Shell shrimp, leaving tails on. Slit shrimp lengthwise along vein, but not completely through. Open shrimp until almost flat; remove vein. Pat shrimp dry with paper towels. Pour oil to a 2-inch depth in a deep-fryer or large saucepan. Heat oil to 375F (190C) or until a 1-inch bread cube turns golden brown in 50 seconds. In a shallow bowl, combine flour, salt, pepper and seasoned salt. In another shallow bowl, beat together egg and water. Dip each shrimp in flour mixture, then beaten egg and finally in bread crumbs. Fry coated shrimp, 3 or 4 at a time, in hot oil until light golden on one side; turn and cook other side. Drain on paper towels. Repeat with remaining shrimp. Serve hot. Makes 16 shrimp.

Lacy Tempura Dinner

Ice-cold water in the batter helps to give that light lacy look typical of tempura.

1 pound large uncooked shrimp or fish fillets, cut into 1-inch strips
1 red or yellow bell pepper, cut into 8 wedges
10 to 12 fresh green beans, ends trimmed
1 small sweet potato, peeled, sliced crosswise
1 medium onion, cut crosswise into 1/2-inch slices

Oil for deep-frying
1 egg, beaten slightly
2/3 cup all-purpose flour
2 tablespoons cornstarch
1/2 teaspoon baking powder
1 cup ice water

Shell shrimp, leaving tails on. Slit shrimp lengthwise along vein, but not completely through. Open shrimp until almost flat; remove vein. Pat vegetables and shrimp dry with paper towels. Pour oil to a 2-inch depth in a deep-fryer or large saucepan. Heat oil to 375F (190C) or until a 1-inch bread cube turns golden brown in 50 seconds. In a medium bowl, combine egg, flour, cornstarch, baking powder and ice water; beat until smooth. Immediately dip prepared vegetables and shrimp or fish into batter. Fry in hot oil until light golden on one side; turn and cook other side. Drain on paper towels. Repeat until all vegetables and shrimp or fish are fried. Serve warm. Makes 5 to 6 servings.

Italian Riviera Submarines

*For a change-of-pace dinner, try this hearty open-faced sandwich
with all the favorite Mediterranean flavors.*

3 large (6-inch) sourdough or French rolls

3 tablespoons red-wine vinegar

1 tablespoon chopped fresh basil

4 anchovies, chopped

1/8 teaspoon black pepper

1 garlic clove, chopped

1/2 cup olive oil or vegetable oil

6 thin slices prosciutto

6 slices fontina or Monterey Jack cheese

1 yellow or green bell pepper, thinly sliced

1 red onion, thinly sliced

2 medium tomatoes, thinly sliced

Green or ripe olives, red onion, yellow pepper and
fresh herbs for garnish, optional

Split rolls lengthwise; make 2 or 3 crosswise cuts on each half, almost through to crust. In a blender or food processor fitted with the metal blade, combine vinegar, basil, anchovies, black pepper and garlic. With machine running, gradually add oil. Generously brush mixture over cut sides of rolls. Arrange prosciutto and cheese on rolls. Top with bell pepper and red onion, then tomatoes. Garnish with olives, red onion, yellow pepper and fresh herbs, if desired. Serve immediately. Makes 6 servings.

Oriental-Style Baby-Back Ribs

Baby-back ribs are smaller and more tender than regular ribs.

2-1/4 pounds baby-back pork ribs

Salt

Pepper

2 tablespoons honey

2 tablespoons soy sauce

1 tablespoon grated fresh ginger

1 garlic clove, crushed

2 tablespoons hoisin sauce

1 tablespoon lemon juice

2 tablespoons finely chopped green onion

Preheat oven to 350F (175C). Cut meat into individual ribs; place in a shallow baking pan. Season with salt and pepper. Cover with foil. Bake in preheated oven 35 to 40 minutes or until almost done. Uncover ribs; increase oven temperature to 425F (220C). Meanwhile, in a medium saucepan, combine honey, soy sauce, ginger, garlic, hoisin sauce, lemon juice and green onion; simmer 5 minutes. Brush tops of cooked ribs with sauce; bake 10 minutes. Turn, brush other side with sauce; bake ribs another 5 minutes or to desired doneness. Makes 20 to 25 rib pieces.

Tasty Oriental Beef Bundles

*So easy to make with refrigerated crescent rolls. Ideal when warm
but may be eaten at room temperature.*

1/2 pound lean ground beef

2 green onions, sliced

1 tablespoon hoisin sauce

1 egg, beaten slightly

1 tablespoon honey

1 tablespoon soy sauce

1 teaspoon grated fresh ginger

1 (8-oz.) package refrigerator crescent rolls

1 tablespoon butter or margarine, melted

2 teaspoons sesame seeds

Preheat oven to 400F (205C). In a medium skillet, cook ground beef, green onions and hoisin sauce, stirring to break up pieces of meat. In a small bowl, combine egg, honey, soy sauce and ginger; add to cooked meat. Cook 1 minute; remove from heat. Unroll crescent-roll dough. Divide dough into 4 rectangles with 2 triangles in each. With fingers, press out perforations. On a lightly floured board, roll out each rectangle to a 6-inch square. Spoon about 6 tablespoons cooked-meat mixture onto each square. Bring up edges of dough to cover filling, pinching together in center to form a bundle. Brush tops with melted butter; sprinkle with sesame seeds. Place bundles on a baking sheet. Bake in preheated oven 8 to 10 minutes or until golden brown. Remove from oven; cool 5 minutes. Makes 4 servings.

Broiled Turkey Kabobs

*Turkey and other poultry are done if juices run clear when pierced
with a fork. Overcooking results in dry kabobs.*

1-1/4 pounds (1/2-inch-thick) turkey-breast steaks

2 tablespoons butter or margarine, melted

1 tablespoon Dijon-style mustard

1 tablespoon Worcestershire sauce

1/4 cup plum jam or preserves

1 teaspoon grated fresh ginger

1 garlic clove, crushed

1 tablespoon lemon juice

1/4 teaspoon salt

1 tablespoon toasted sesame seeds

Cut turkey into 1-1/4-inch squares. Using 4 (6-inch) skewers, thread 4 or 5 squares on each skewer. Place skewers in a shallow baking pan. Brush turkey with melted butter. In a small bowl, combine mustard, Worcestershire sauce, plum jam, ginger, garlic, lemon juice and salt. Broil turkey kabobs 4 to 5 inches from heat source 2 minutes. Brush kabobs with sauce; broil 1 to 2 minutes or until done. Brush with sauce again. Sprinkle lightly with sesame seeds. Serve hot. Makes 4 servings.

Roast Pork & Apple Boboli

Boboli is an Italian-type bread that's often used as a prepared base for pizza. We enjoy using it for this roast pork combination.

1 tablespoon vegetable oil
1 small onion, thinly sliced
1 teaspoon Dijon-style mustard
1/2 teaspoon grated fresh ginger
1 tablespoon orange juice
1/2 teaspoon grated orange peel
1/2 teaspoon chili powder

1 teaspoon brown sugar
1/8 teaspoon salt
1 medium apple, thinly sliced
6 to 8 ounces thinly sliced roast pork
1 (8-oz.) package Boboli bread shells, warmed
    (two 6-inch shells)

In 10-inch skillet, heat oil; stir in onion. Heat until onion is limp. In small bowl, combine mustard, ginger, orange juice, orange peel, chili powder, brown sugar and salt. Add apple and sauce mixture to onion. Cover and cook over low heat until apples are soft. Add pork; cook until heated. Spoon half of cooked mixture into each bread shell. Quarter each for ease in eating. Makes 2 large individual servings of 4 quarters each; or 4 snack servings of 2 quarters each.

Flaky Beef Turnovers

It's important to cut potatoes and steak into very small pieces, so they get done by the time the pastry is brown.

6 ounces boneless beef top round or rib-eye
    steak
2 small potatoes, peeled, diced
1/2 of a (1.25-oz.) envelope dry onion-soup mix
    (about 3 tablespoons)

2 tablespoons ketchup
1 teaspoon Worcestershire sauce
1 tablespoon chopped fresh parsley
6 frozen puff-pastry shells (one 10-oz. package)

Preheat oven to 400F (205C). Trim beef; discard fat. Cut beef into cubes no larger than 1/2 inch. In a medium bowl, combine beef, potatoes, soup mix, ketchup, Worcestershire sauce and parsley. On a lightly floured board, roll out each pastry shell to a 7-inch circle. Spoon equal amounts or about 1/4 cup meat mixture on each rolled-out shell. Brush edges with water. Fold over; press with tines of a fork to seal. Cut several slits in top of each. Place on a baking sheet. Bake in preheated oven 20 to 25 minutes or until golden brown. Serve hot. Makes 6 turnovers.

Crumb-Coated Zucchini Diagonals

*For variety, use cheese-flavored crackers and leave out the
Parmesan cheese.*

3 medium zucchini
1 egg, beaten slightly
1/4 teaspoon salt
1/8 teaspoon pepper

1/4 cup dairy sour cream
20 round butter-flavored crackers, crushed
2 tablespoons grated Parmesan cheese

Preheat oven to 375F (190C). Cut zucchini in 1/2-inch diagonal slices. In a small bowl, combine egg, salt, pepper and sour cream. In another small bowl, combine cracker crumbs and cheese. Dip each zucchini slice in egg mixture, then roll in cracker crumbs. Place in a shallow baking pan. Bake in preheated oven 20 to 25 minutes or until zucchini is tender. Serve hot. Makes 20 to 25 slices, depending on size of zucchini.

Smoky Cheese-Potato Slices

*Cheese spread is quite salty, so it's not necessary to add salt
unless you're a real salt enthusiast.*

3 medium baking potatoes (5 to 6 oz. each)
1/2 cup smoky Cheddar-cheese spread
3 tablespoons finely chopped sun-dried tomatoes
   in oil

1/2 teaspoon Worcestershire sauce
Finely chopped fresh parsley

Preheat oven to 425F (220C). Bake potatoes 40 minutes or until barely tender; cool to room temperature. Do not peel. Slice cooked potatoes crosswise into 1/2-inch slices. Arrange potato slices in a shallow baking pan. In a small bowl, combine cheese spread, tomatoes and Worcestershire sauce. Top each potato slice with about 1/2 tablespoon cheese mixture. Broil 4 to 5 inches from heat source 1 to 1-1/2 minutes or until bubbly. Sprinkle with parsley. Serve warm. Makes 15 to 18 slices.

Tip
You will find sun-dried tomatoes in small plastic bags or in jars of olive oil. Those in the bags have a look of a dried fruit or vegetable, while those in oil are soft and moist. Recipes in this book calling for sun-dried tomatoes use the ones packed in oil.

Crunchy Eggplant Sticks

If you have trouble coating with mayonnaise, use a pastry brush.
Lightly brush mayonnaise all over eggplant strips; then roll strips in
crumbs.

1 medium eggplant	**2 cups crushed corn chips**
3/4 cup mayonnaise	

Preheat oven to 375F (190C). Peel eggplant; cut into strips about 1/2 inch thick and 1 inch wide. Cut each strip in half crosswise to about 2-1/2 to 3 inches, depending on length of eggplant. Coat all sides with mayonnaise; then roll in crushed corn chips. Place coated strips in a shallow baking pan. Bake in preheated oven 15 minutes or until eggplant is done. Serve warm. Makes 35 to 40 sticks.

Garden-Path Dip for Pita Wedges

You'll love the combination of vegetables. For a change, try it with
corn chips or tortilla chips.

1-1/2 pounds banana squash	**1 garlic clove, crushed**
2 tablespoons vegetable oil	**1 tablespoon white-wine vinegar**
1 onion, chopped	**2 tablespoons capers**
1 carrot, peeled, grated	**1/2 teaspoon salt**
2 celery stalks, chopped	**1/4 teaspoon pepper**
2 small tomatoes, peeled, seeded, chopped	**1/4 teaspoon dried leaf marjoram, crushed**
2 tablespoons finely chopped fresh parsley	**Toasted wedges of pita bread rounds**

Remove peel from squash; cut into 1/2-inch cubes. In a large skillet, heat oil. Add squash, onion and carrot; sauté 2 to 3 minutes. Stir in celery, tomatoes, parsley, garlic, vinegar, capers, salt, pepper and marjoram. Cover and cook on medium-low 15 to 20 minutes, stirring occasionally. Serve as a dip for toasted wedges of pita bread. Makes about 4 cups dip.

Herb-Parmesan Muffins

Using fresh herbs results in the best flavor.

2 eggs, beaten slightly
1 cup milk
1/4 cup vegetable oil
1/4 cup finely chopped sun-dried tomatoes in oil
2 cups all-purpose flour
2 teaspoons baking powder

3/4 teaspoon salt
1/2 teaspoon baking soda
1 tablespoon finely chopped fresh basil
1 tablespoon finely chopped fresh oregano
1 tablespoon finely chopped fresh parsley
1/4 cup (3/4 oz.) grated Parmesan cheese

Preheat oven to 400F (205C). Grease 12 (2-1/2- to 3-inch) muffin cups. In a small bowl, combine eggs, milk, oil and tomatoes. In a large bowl, combine flour, baking powder, baking soda, basil, oregano, parsley and 2 tablespoons Parmesan cheese. Stir in egg mixture. Spoon mixture into prepared muffin cups. Sprinkle with remaining 2 tablespoons Parmesan cheese. Bake in preheated oven 20 to 22 minutes or until golden brown. Remove from oven. Loosen from sides; remove to a cooling rack. Serve warm. Makes 12 muffins.

Variation
Mini Herb-Parmesan Muffins: Use 1-3/4-inch miniature muffin cups and reduce baking time to 12 to 15 minutes. Makes about 36 miniature muffins.

Jalapeño Corn Muffins

*Jalapeño pepper lends a pleasant "hot" touch. California chilies
may be substituted for a milder-flavored muffin.*

1 egg, beaten slightly
1/2 cup milk
2 tablespoons vegetable oil
1 cup (4 oz.) finely chopped Monterey Jack
   cheese
1 (8-oz.) can cream-style corn

2 tablespoons chopped green onion
1 jalapeño pepper, finely chopped
1/4 teaspoon baking soda
1/4 teaspoon salt
1 cup yellow cornmeal

Preheat oven to 400F (205C). Grease 12 (2-1/2- to 3-inch) muffin cups. In a medium bowl, combine egg, milk, oil, cheese, corn, green onion and jalapeño pepper. Stir in baking soda, salt and cornmeal. Spoon into prepared muffin cups. Bake in preheated oven 20 to 22 minutes or until golden brown. Remove from oven. Loosen from sides; invert on a cooling rack. Serve warm. Makes 12 muffins.

Chunky Herbed Bread Sticks

It's fun to make your own bread sticks. These are thicker than those available in the markets—more like a hearty roll.

1 (1/4-oz.) package active dry yeast (about 1 tablespoon)
1 cup warm water (110F/45C)
1 teaspoon sugar
1/4 teaspoon dried leaf oregano, crushed
1 teaspoon salt

1/4 teaspoon dried leaf rosemary, crushed
2 tablespoons vegetable oil
2-3/4 to 3 cups all-purpose flour
1 egg white
1 tablespoon water
Sesame seeds, poppy seeds or coarse salt

Grease a large baking sheet; set aside. In a medium bowl, dissolve yeast in warm water. Let stand about 5 minutes. Stir in sugar, oregano, salt, rosemary, oil and 1 cup flour. Beat 2 minutes or until well blended. Add enough additional flour to make a soft dough. Turn out dough on a lightly floured board. Knead about 15 times or until dough is fairly firm and smooth. Pat dough to a 9-inch square. With a long sharp knife, cut dough in half; then each half into 6 strips, approximately 4-1/2" x 1-1/2". Using your fingers, gently roll each dough piece into a rope about 8 inches long. Arrange ropes, about 1 inch apart, on prepared baking sheet. In a small bowl, combine egg white and 1 tablespoon water. Brush ropes with egg-white mixture. Sprinkle with seeds or coarse salt. Cover and let rise in a warm place 30 minutes. Preheat oven to 425F (220C). Bake in preheated oven 10 to 15 minutes or until golden brown. Cool on a rack. Makes 12 bread sticks.

Crab & Brie in Puff Pastry

What elegant little bundles! Frozen puff pastry offers a shortcut to a recipe that usually takes hours to produce.

1/3 cup slivered almonds
1 tablespoon butter or margarine
4 ounces crabmeat
2 teaspoons dry vermouth

1 sheet frozen puff pastry, thawed
1 egg, beaten
1/2 pound Brie cheese, cut into 1-inch cubes

Preheat oven to 425F (220C). In a small skillet, combine almonds and butter. Stir over medium heat until almonds are golden; set aside. In a small bowl, combine crabmeat and vermouth. On a lightly floured board, roll puff pastry sheet to an 18" x 14" rectangle. Cut a 1/2-inch strip from the 14-inch side; cover and set aside. This is for bundle ties. Cut remaining sheet into 12 (4-1/2-inch) squares. Place 2 teaspoons crabmeat mixture in center of each square. Brush edges with beaten egg. Top with a cube of Brie and 1 teaspoon toasted almonds. Bring opposite corners of pastry up around filling to form a bag or parcel. Pinch firmly as close to filling as possible; flare corners gently. Cut reserved pastry strip into 4 (1/8-inch-wide) strips, then crosswise into thirds. Wrap a strip around neck of each bag overlapping to form the tie. Brush a small amount of beaten egg where strip overlaps to secure. Brush tops and sides of parcels with beaten egg. Place on an ungreased baking sheet; refrigerate at least 20 minutes. Preheat oven to 425F (220C). Bake in preheated oven 10 minutes or until golden brown. Serve hot. Makes 12 servings.

Roquefort-Onion Rolls

*Those who think Roquefort dressing is limited to green salads will
be amazed how great it is in this recipe.*

1/3 cup refrigerated thick Roquefort-cheese
    dressing or thick blue-cheese dressing
1 cup (4 oz.) shredded Monterey Jack cheese

2 tablespoons finely chopped green onion
2 tablespoons butter or margarine, melted
4 Kaiser rolls or hamburger buns, split

In a small bowl, combine Roquefort dressing, cheese, green onion and butter. Spread mixture on cut side of roll halves. Place rolls, cut-side up, on a broiler pan. Broil 4 to 5 inches from heat source 2 to 3 minutes or until hot and bubbly. Serve warm. Makes 8 servings.

Dilly Brioche with Jarlsberg

*Small brioche pans give an elegant look for special occasions. If
they aren't available, use custard cups or muffin pans.*

1 (1/4-oz.) package active dry yeast (about 1
    tablespoon)
1/2 cup warm water (110F/45C)
3 eggs, beaten slightly
1/2 cup butter or margarine, cut into 8 pieces,
    room temperature
2 tablespoons sugar

1 teaspoon salt
3 to 3-1/2 cups all-purpose flour
1 teaspoon dried dill weed
1 cup (4 oz.) shredded Jarlsberg cheese
1 egg yolk, beaten slightly
1 tablespoon milk
Additional dill weed

In a large bowl, dissolve yeast in warm water. Let stand about 5 minutes. Stir in 3 eggs, butter, sugar, salt and 1 cup flour. Beat with an electric mixer 2 minutes or until well blended. Stir in 1 teaspoon dill weed, cheese and enough additional flour to make a soft pliable dough. Turn out dough on a lightly floured board. Knead dough 7 to 8 minutes or until dough is elastic. Clean and grease bowl. Place dough in greased bowl, turning to grease all sides. Cover and let rise in a warm place until doubled in bulk, about 45 minutes. Punch down dough; let stand 5 minutes. Grease 16 individual brioche pans or other small baking pans. Divide dough into 16 pieces. Pinch off a small amount of dough, about the size of a large grape, from each of the 16 pieces. Shape each of the small pieces like a teardrop. Shape the large pieces of dough into balls. Place one ball in each greased pan or cup. Press center of each to form a depression about 1/2 inch deep. Insert a teardrop-shaped dough piece, small-end down, in each. Cover and let rise until doubled in bulk, about 45 minutes. Preheat oven to 425F (220C). In a small bowl, combine egg yolk and milk. Gently brush tops of brioche with egg-yolk glaze. Sprinkle with additional dill weed. Bake in preheated oven 10 minutes or until golden brown. Serve warm. Makes 16 rolls.

Dessert Samplers

Dazzle the most discriminating dessert lovers with one of our dessert samplers. In addition to being delicious, they can be picked up and eaten with your fingers. Either they're individual servings or can be cut into bars or wedges that can be picked up. This means that many of them can be taken to tailgate parties, tucked into packed lunches for work or school, or eaten on-the-run when time is limited.

We've combined popular ingredients to create tantalizing flavors. Who can resist Upside-Down Chocolate Cheesecakes, made with everyone's favorite chocolate sandwich cookies? Or how about cheesecakes combining chocolate, almonds and marshmallows for a rocky-road treat.

For individual desserts, we've used a variety of miniature baking pans. Muffin pans in varying sizes are practical all-purpose containers. Standard-size muffin pans are made with either six or twelve cups 2-1/2 to 3 inches in diameter. Mini-muffin pans range from 1-3/4 to 2 inches in diameter. Size is indicated for each recipe. If you use a size larger or smaller than indicated, adjust the baking time accordingly.

The 6-ounce custard cup is another favorite container for making individual desserts. Small fluted containers similar to miniature brioche pans and 3-inch quiche pans are also handy to use. After you fill small pans, place them in a large shallow baking pan for ease in taking them in and out of the oven.

Macadamia-Praline Pizza

*Not a real pizza, but a superb dessert that's a cross between a
praline and a pecan pie. Don't be surprised if the mixture bubbles
up when cream is added to filling. (Photo on previous pages.)*

1/2 cup butter or margarine, room temperature
1/2 cup granulated sugar
1 egg
2 cups all-purpose flour
1-1/4 cups lightly packed brown sugar

3/4 cup butter or margarine
2 tablespoons honey
1 cup macadamia nuts
3 tablespoons whipping cream

Preheat oven to 375F (190C). Line bottom of a 12-inch pizza pan with parchment paper. In a medium bowl, cream 1/2 cup butter and granulated sugar until light and fluffy. Beat in egg; then blend in flour. Pat mixture onto bottom and side of lined pizza pan. Bake in preheated oven 18 minutes. In a medium saucepan, combine brown sugar, 3/4 cup butter and honey; cook over low heat, stirring occasionally, until butter melts. Bring to a boil over medium heat; remove from heat. Stir in macadamia nuts and whipping cream. Immediately spread mixture over hot, partially baked crust. Bake 8 to 10 minutes or until bubbly. Remove from oven; cut into 10 to 12 wedges. Makes 1 (12-inch) pizza.

Easy Apple Turnovers

*A quick and easy way to make turnovers. If you have a favorite
pastry recipe, use amount for a two-crust (9-inch) pie instead of
refrigerated pie crust.*

1 (15-oz.) package refrigerated pre-rolled pie crust
2 cooking apples, peeled, chopped
3 tablespoons chopped walnuts
1 tablespoon all-purpose flour

1/2 cup sugar
1/2 teaspoon ground cinnamon
1/4 teaspoon ground nutmeg
1/4 cup butter or margarine, melted

Preheat oven to 375F (190C). Divide each circle of pie crust into quarters along fold lines. On a lightly floured board, roll each piece into a 6-inch circle. In a medium bowl, combine apples, walnuts and flour. In another small bowl, combine sugar, cinnamon and nutmeg. Spoon about 1/4 cup apple mixture in center of each circle of pastry. Sprinkle about 2 teaspoons sugar mixture over apples on each pastry round. Fold dough in half over apples; press edges with a fork to seal. Dip both sides of each turnover in melted butter. Place buttered turnovers in a 15" x 10" jelly-roll pan. Sprinkle remaining sugar mixture over turnovers. Bake in preheated oven 15 to 20 minutes or until golden brown. Serve warm. Makes 8 turnovers.

Peanut-Butter Mini Loaves

We used small loaf pans that we bought in a kitchen shop. If you have miniature round pans, they can be used for individual servings or cake-for-two.

1/3 cup butter or margarine, room temperature
3/4 cup sugar
1 egg
1 teaspoon vanilla extract
1-1/3 cups all-purpose flour

1-1/4 teaspoons baking powder
1/4 teaspoon salt
2/3 cup milk
15 miniature candy peanut-butter cups
1/3 cup chopped peanuts

Preheat oven to 350F (175C). Grease 6 (3-1/2" x 2-1/2") loaf pans. In a medium bowl, combine butter, sugar, egg, vanilla, flour, baking powder, salt and milk; beat 3 minutes. Cut each peanut-butter cup into 4 pieces; stir into batter. Spoon batter into prepared loaf pans. Bake in preheated oven 20 to 25 minutes or until top springs back when touched with your finger tip. Remove from oven; cool in pans 5 minutes. Remove from pans; cool on a rack. Spread Chocolate-Peanut Topping over top and sides of cakes. Sprinkle tops with chopped peanuts. Makes 6 miniature loaves.

Chocolate-Peanut Topping:

6 ounces semisweet chocolate,
   broken up

2 tablespoons butter or margarine
2 tablespoons light corn syrup

In a small saucepan, combine chocolate, butter and corn syrup. Stir over low heat until melted.

White-Chocolate-Raspberry Cups

You can remove chocolate shells from custard cups as soon as they are firm. Keep them refrigerated, then fill with berries immediately before serving. (Photo on cover.)

3 ounces white chocolate, coarsely chopped
2 tablespoons butter or margarine
1 tablespoon milk
1/4 teaspoon vanilla extract

1/2 cup toasted blanched almonds, chopped
1-1/2 cups sifted powdered sugar
1-1/4 to 1-1/2 cups fresh or frozen raspberries

In a small saucepan, combine white chocolate, butter and milk. Stir over low heat until chocolate melts; remove from heat. Immediately stir in vanilla, almonds and powdered sugar. Press mixture onto bottoms and about 1-1/2 inches up sides of 4 or 5 (6-ounce) custard cups. Refrigerate at least 1 hour or until firm. Wrap outside of chilled custard cups with a warm towel. Loosen by inserting a small spatula between custard cup and white-chocolate lining. To serve, fill each chocolate shell with raspberries. Makes 4 or 5 servings.

Hawaiian Cheese Tarts

If you are fond of papaya, add more than one slice to each tart.

2 cups flaked coconut
1/4 cup butter or margarine, melted
1/2 cup sugar
2 eggs
1 (8-oz.) package cream cheese, room
    temperature

1/2 cup dairy sour cream
2 tablespoons all-purpose flour
1/4 cup finely chopped macadamia nuts
1 (8-oz.) can crushed pineapple, drained
Papaya slices

In a medium bowl, combine coconut and butter. Press mixture onto bottoms of 12 (3- or 4-inch) tart pans or quiche pans. Refrigerate while making filling. Preheat oven to 350F (175C). In a medium bowl, cream sugar, eggs and cheese. Blend in sour cream, flour and macadamia nuts. With the back of a spoon, press excess liquid from pineapple. Reserve juice for another purpose. Add pineapple to cheese mixture. Spoon into lined pans. Place pans on a 15" x 10" jelly-roll pan. Bake in preheated oven 20 minutes or until firm. Remove from oven; cool on a rack. Run a small spatula around edges to loosen. Top with papaya slices. Makes 12 servings.

Raspberry-Hazelnut Stacks

They're at their very best when freshly baked, but are still delicious when kept in a closed container and served several days later. (Photo on page 89.)

1/2 cup hazelnuts
1 cup butter or margarine
1/2 cup granulated sugar
2 cups all-purpose flour

1/2 teaspoon vanilla extract
1/2 cup raspberry jam
Powdered sugar

Preheat oven to 400F (205C). Place hazelnuts in a shallow baking pan. Bake in preheated oven 6 minutes or until skins begin to crack. Wrap nuts in a clean towel; let stand 2 minutes. Rub nuts briskly with towel to remove most of the dark skins. Grind toasted nuts in a blender or food processor fitted with the metal blade until nuts are the texture of coarse bread crumbs. In a medium bowl, cream butter and granulated sugar until light and fluffy. Add ground hazelnuts, flour and vanilla; blend well. Form dough into 2 rolls about 5-1/2 inches long and 2 inches in diameter. Wrap rolls in plastic wrap; refrigerate at least 2 hours. Preheat oven to 375F (190C). Cut dough into 1/4-inch-thick slices. Place on large baking sheets. Bake in preheated oven 10 minutes or until light golden brown. Cool; spread 1/2 the cookies with jam. Top with remaining cookies. Sprinkle with powdered sugar. Makes about 22 sandwich cookies.

Hazelnut-Cream-Cheese Envelopes

They're small, but have a special appeal for all hazelnut fans.

1 (3-oz.) package cream cheese, room
   temperature
3 tablespoons butter or margarine
2 tablespoons sugar
3 tablespoons milk

1-1/8 cups all-purpose flour
1/2 teaspoon baking powder
1/8 teaspoon salt
15 whole hazelnuts, toasted
1 tablespoon sugar

Preheat oven to 375F (190C). In a large bowl, beat together cream cheese, butter, 2 tablespoons sugar and milk until smooth. Stir in flour, baking powder and salt. Press dough together to form a ball. On a lightly floured board, roll out dough to 15" x 9". Cut into 15 (3-inch) squares. Spoon about 2 teaspoons cooled Hazelnut Filling in center of each square on a diagonal almost to edges. Bring 2 opposite corners of pastry over filling to center. Overlap slightly to resemble an envelope. Repeat with remaining squares. Press 1 whole hazelnut in center of each envelope. Place envelopes on an ungreased baking sheet; sprinkle each with about 1/8 teaspoon sugar. Bake in preheated oven 12 to 15 minutes or until edges just begin to brown. Makes 15 servings.

Hazelnut Filling:

2/3 cup hazelnuts, toasted, with most
   of the skins removed
1/3 cup sugar

1-1/2 tablespoons hazelnut liqueur
1/3 cup half and half

In a food processor fitted with the metal blade, finely chop hazelnuts. Add 1/3 cup sugar, liqueur and half and half. Process until almost smooth. Pour into a small saucepan; cook and stir over low heat until mixture begins to boil and thickens slightly. Cover and cool in a refrigerator.

Tip
To toast hazelnuts, place in a shallow baking pan.
Bake in a 400F (205C) oven 6 minutes or until skins
begin to crack. Wrap nuts in a clean towel; let stand
2 minutes. Rub nuts briskly with towel to remove
most of the dark skins.

Coconut-Orange Cheesecake Cups

Placing the muffin pan on a hot dish towel will aid in removing cheesecakes.

1-1/2 cups crushed crisp coconut cookies (about 9 cookies)
1/4 cup butter or margarine, melted
1 teaspoon unflavored gelatin powder
3 tablespoons sugar
1/4 cup orange juice
1 egg, beaten slightly

1/2 cup (4 oz.) small-curd cottage cheese
1/4 teaspoon grated orange peel
1 teaspoon grated fresh ginger
1/4 cup dairy sour cream
Fresh orange slices for garnish, optional
Toasted coconut for garnish, optional

In a small bowl, combine crushed cookies and butter. Press mixture onto bottoms and sides of 12 (1-3/4-inch) miniature muffin cups. Refrigerate while preparing filling. In a medium saucepan, combine gelatin and sugar; stir in orange juice and egg. Cook over medium heat, stirring until slightly thickened. Remove from heat; refrigerate until partially set. In a food processor fitted with the metal blade, combine cottage cheese, orange peel and ginger; process until nearly smooth. Stir in sour cream; combine with orange-juice mixture. Spoon into crumb-lined muffin cups. Chill until firm. Run a small spatula around edge of each cheesecake to remove. Garnish with fresh orange slices or toasted coconut, if desired. Makes 12 miniature cheesecakes.

Rocky-Road Cheesecake Cups

Double chocolate for all chocoholics! It takes about 36 thin chocolate wafers to make enough crumbs for the crust.

2 cups chocolate wafer crumbs (about 36 cookies)
3 tablespoons butter or margarine, melted
1 tablespoon sugar
1 (8-oz.) package cream cheese, room temperature
1/3 cup sugar

3 tablespoons unsweetened cocoa powder
2 eggs
1/2 cup dairy sour cream
1/2 teaspoon vanilla extract
1/2 cup miniature marshmallows
1/4 cup chopped almonds

In a medium bowl, combine wafer crumbs, melted butter and 1 tablespoon sugar. Press onto bottoms and sides of 14 (2-1/2- to 3-inch) muffin cups or 6-ounce custard cups. Refrigerate while preparing filling. Preheat oven to 350F (175C). In a medium bowl, beat cream cheese to soften; blend in 1/3 cup sugar, cocoa powder, eggs, sour cream and vanilla. Stir in marshmallows and almonds. Spoon into crumb-lined cups. Bake in preheated oven 20 to 22 minutes or until set. Remove from oven; cool. Run a small spatula around edge of each cheesecake to remove. Makes 14 individual cheesecakes.

Cream & Sugar-Stuffed Strawberries, page 109, and Coconut-Orange Cheesecake Cups, above.

Upside-Down Chocolate Cheesecakes

Everybody's favorite chocolate cookie gives flavor to these little cheesecakes.

1 (8-oz.) package cream cheese, room temperature
1 cup (8 oz.) small-curd cottage cheese
1/2 cup sugar

2 eggs
1/2 teaspoon vanilla extract
1 tablespoon all-purpose flour
8 creme-filled chocolate-sandwich cookies

Preheat oven to 350F (175C). Grease 8 (6-ounce) custard cups. In a medium bowl, beat together cream cheese and cottage cheese until almost smooth. Beat in sugar, eggs, vanilla and flour. Open 4 cookies; place one cookie piece, frosted-side up, in bottom of each prepared custard cup. Coarsely chop remaining 4 cookies; fold into cheese mixture. Spoon mixture over cookies in custard cups. Place filled cups on a 15" x 10" jelly-roll pan. Bake in preheated oven 25 minutes or until firm. Cool in cups 10 minutes. Run a small spatula around edge of each cheesecake; invert onto a tray. Refrigerate until ready to serve. Makes 8 individual cheesecakes.

Banana-Praline Cheesecakes

These individual cheesecakes are easier to remove from muffin cups after they are chilled.

2 cups vanilla wafer crumbs (about 40 wafers)
1/2 cup butter or margarine, melted
2 tablespoons granulated sugar
1 (8-oz.) package cream cheese, room temperature
1/2 cup lightly packed brown sugar

1 tablespoon all-purpose flour
2 eggs
1 ripe banana, mashed
1 tablespoon rum
1/4 cup chopped pecans

In a medium bowl, combine wafer crumbs, butter and granulated sugar. Press mixture onto bottoms and up sides almost to top of 12 (2-1/2- to 3-inch) muffin cups; refrigerate crumb-lined cups. Preheat oven to 350F (175C). In a medium bowl, combine cream cheese and brown sugar until smooth. Add flour, eggs, banana and rum; blend well. Stir in pecans. Spoon into chilled crumb-lined cups. Bake in preheated oven 20 to 25 minutes or until firm. Remove from oven; cool in pans. Run a small spatula around edge of each cheesecake; remove from pan. Makes 12 individual cheesecakes.

Frozen Deviled Angel-Food Sandwiches

You can take a short-cut on this one by substituting rocky-road ice cream for chocolate ice cream, marshmallows and nuts.

2 cups miniature marshmallows
1/4 cup milk
1 (6-oz.) angel-food loaf cake

1 pint chocolate ice cream
1/2 cup chopped pecans
2 teaspoons unsweetened cocoa powder

In a small saucepan, combine marshmallows and milk over very low heat, stirring constantly. When marshmallows are about half dissolved, remove from heat; set aside to cool. Stir or whisk several times while cooling. Cut cake crosswise into 16 slices; set aside. When marshmallow mixture is cold, soften ice cream slightly; stir in nuts. Then stir marshmallow mixture into ice cream just enough to create a swirled effect. If ice-cream mixture is too soft, return to freezer about 30 minutes. Spread about 1/4 cup ice-cream mixture on a slice of cake. Top ice cream with another cake slice, forming a sandwich. Very lightly dust sandwich with cocoa powder. Place in freezer. Continue with remaining cake slices and ice cream. Serve when sandwich fillings are firm. Or, wrap each sandwich in foil or plastic wrap. Then place in a freezer bag, seal and store until needed. Makes 8 servings.

Chocolate-Buttercream Ladyfinger Sandwiches

So impressive that your friends will think they took hours to make. Chop almonds almost as fine as bread crumbs so they'll go through a pastry bag. (Photo on cover.)

6 tablespoons butter or margarine, room temperature
1-1/2 cups sifted powdered sugar
1 egg yolk
1/2 teaspoon vanilla extract

3 tablespoons unsweetened cocoa powder
1 tablespoon finely chopped toasted almonds
12 ladyfingers, split lengthwise
Powdered sugar

In a medium bowl, beat butter until very light and creamy. Gradually add 1-1/2 cups sugar, beating constantly until fluffy. Beat in egg yolk, then vanilla and cocoa powder. Fold in almonds. Fit a pastry bag with a large star-tip; fill bag with chocolate mixture. Pipe mixture onto cut side of bottom half of each ladyfinger; top with other half. Sprinkle each ladyfinger with powdered sugar. Serve immediately or refrigerate and serve later. Makes 12 servings.

Cinnamon-Apple-Pecan Bars

A variation of an apple recipe that's been a standard in our family for years.

1-1/4 cups all-purpose flour

1/4 cup granulated sugar

1/2 cup butter or margarine

1 egg

3/4 cup lightly packed brown sugar

1/2 teaspoon ground cinnamon

1/8 teaspoon ground nutmeg

3/4 cup all-purpose flour

1/4 teaspoon salt

1/4 cup butter or margarine, melted

1 cup finely chopped, peeled apple

1/4 cup chopped pecans

Preheat oven to 375F (190C). In a medium bowl, combine 1-1/4 cups flour, granulated sugar and butter. With a pastry blender or fork, blend until mixture resembles coarse crumbs. Press mixture onto bottom of an 8-inch-square baking pan. Bake in preheated oven 20 to 22 minutes or until mixture begins to brown around edges. Meanwhile, in a medium bowl, beat egg slightly. Beat in brown sugar, cinnamon, nutmeg, 3/4 cup flour, salt and melted butter. Stir in apples and pecans. Spoon over partially baked crust. Return to oven; bake 25 minutes or until top is firm and starts to shrink away from sides. Remove from oven; cool on a rack. Drizzle with Glaze. Cut into 1-1/2-inch bars. Makes about 25 bars.

Glaze:

1/2 cup powdered sugar

1-1/2 teaspoons milk

1/4 teaspoon vanilla extract

In a small bowl, combine powdered sugar, milk and vanilla.

Apple-Spice Diagonals

Apricot jam is a good substitute if apple butter is not your favorite.

1/2 cup butter or margarine, room temperature

1/4 cup lightly packed brown sugar

1/2 teaspoon vanilla extract

1/4 teaspoon ground nutmeg

1/4 teaspoon ground ginger

1-1/4 cups all-purpose flour

1/4 cup apple butter

1/2 cup sifted powdered sugar

2 to 3 teaspoons milk

Preheat oven to 350F (175C). In a large bowl, cream butter and brown sugar until fluffy. Beat in vanilla, nutmeg and ginger. Stir in flour. Divide dough into thirds. On a lightly floured board, use your hands to roll each dough piece into a 9-inch rope. Place ropes, 3 inches apart, on a large baking sheet. With the handle of a wooden spoon or your finger tip, make a 1/2-inch indentation or trench down center of each rope. Fill indentation with apple butter. Bake in preheated oven 20 minutes or until golden. Remove from oven; cool on baking sheet. In a small bowl, combine powdered sugar and enough milk to give a drizzling consistency. Drizzle glaze from the tip of a teaspoon in a zigzag pattern over top of cooled cookies. When icing is set, cut diagonally into 1-inch cookies. Makes about 24 cookies.

Mississippi Mud Bars

*Gently swirl partially melted marshmallows and chocolate frosting
to create a "muddy" effect.*

1/2 cup butter or margarine, room temperature
1 cup granulated sugar
2 eggs
1/2 teaspoon vanilla extract
2 tablespoons unsweetened cocoa powder
1/4 cup chopped pecans
1/2 cup flaked coconut

3/4 cup all-purpose flour
1/4 cup butter or margarine, melted
2 cups sifted powdered sugar
3 tablespoons unsweetened cocoa powder
1/2 teaspoon vanilla extract
3 tablespoons milk
1-1/2 cups miniature marshmallows

Preheat oven to 350F(175C). Grease a 9-inch-square baking pan. In a large bowl, beat 1/2 cup butter, granulated sugar, eggs and 1/2 teaspoon vanilla until fluffy. Stir in 2 tablespoons cocoa powder, pecans, coconut and flour until well blended. Spread in prepared pan. Bake in preheated oven 20 to 25 minutes or until crust leaves the sides of pan. While bars bake, beat 1/4 cup melted butter, powdered sugar, 3 tablespoons cocoa powder, 1/2 teaspoon vanilla and milk until smooth. Remove bars from oven. Immediately top with marshmallows. Return to oven for 1 minute to soften marshmallows. Gently spread chocolate-frosting mixture over softened marshmallows. Swirl with a spatula to give a marbled effect. Cool; cut into 1-1/2- to 1-3/4-inch squares. Makes 20 to 25 bars.

Praline Squares

*For all lovers of pralines! The double dose of brown sugar makes
this one a winner.*

2 eggs
3/4 cup lightly packed light-brown sugar
3/4 cup lightly packed dark-brown sugar
1/2 cup butter or margarine, room temperature
1 teaspoon vanilla extract
1/4 teaspoon baking soda
1/2 teaspoon baking powder

1/4 teaspoon salt
1-1/2 cups all-purpose flour
1 cup coarsely chopped pecans
2 tablespoons butter
1 cup sifted powdered sugar
1/2 teaspoon vanilla extract
2 to 3 teaspoons milk

Preheat oven to 350F (175C). Grease a 13" x 9" baking pan. In a large bowl, beat eggs until light colored. Beat in light- and dark-brown sugar, 1/2 cup butter and 1 teaspoon vanilla. Add baking soda, baking powder, salt and flour; beat until smooth. Stir in chopped pecans. Spread in prepared baking pan. Bake in preheated oven 30 minutes or until it begins to shrink from sides of pan. Remove from oven; cool in pan. Heat 2 tablespoons butter in a small pan until it begins to turn amber colored. Remove from heat; stir in powdered sugar, 1/2 teaspoon vanilla and enough milk to give a drizzling consistency. Drizzle glaze from the tip of a teaspoon in a zigzag pattern over top of cooled bars. Cut into 2-inch squares. Makes about 24 bars.

◆

Banana-Fruit Chews

For a different look, drizzle the glaze with the tip of a teaspoon over cookies. This kind of decoration holds its shape better if cookies are completely cool.

1/2 cup vegetable shortening
3/4 cup lightly packed brown sugar
1 egg
1 medium banana, mashed (about 1/2 cup)
1/2 teaspoon ground cinnamon
1/4 teaspoon ground mace
1 teaspoon baking powder
1/2 teaspoon baking soda

1/2 teaspoon salt
1-1/4 cups all-purpose flour
1/2 cup regular or quick-cooking rolled oats
1 teaspoon grated orange peel
1/2 cup dried fruit morsels, page 20
1/2 cup chopped walnuts
Additional dried fruit morsels, page 20

Preheat oven to 375F (190C). In a large bowl, beat shortening, brown sugar and egg until fluffy. Beat in banana, cinnamon, mace, baking powder, baking soda, salt and flour. Stir in rolled oats, orange peel, fruit morsels and nuts. Drop by heaping teaspoons onto large ungreased baking sheets. Bake in preheated oven 10 to 12 minutes. Remove from oven; cool on a rack about 10 minutes. Dip tops of lukewarm cookies into Orange Glaze. Sprinkle with dried fruit morsels. Makes about 25 cookies.

Orange Glaze:

1 cup powdered sugar
4 to 5 teaspoons orange juice

In a small bowl, combine powdered sugar and enough orange juice to form a smooth glaze.

White-Chocolate Macaroon Bars

They won't win a prize for beauty, but they're the very best tasting! Be sure to use sweetened condensed milk, not evaporated milk.

1-1/2 cups all-purpose flour
1/3 cup sifted powdered sugar
3/4 cup butter or margarine
1 egg, beaten slightly
1 (14-oz.) can sweetened condensed milk

1 teaspoon vanilla extract
1/2 cup chopped cashews
1/2 cup flaked coconut
4 ounces white-chocolate pieces (about 2/3 cup)

Preheat oven to 350F (175C). In a medium bowl, combine flour, powdered sugar and butter. With a pastry blender or fork, blend until mixture resembles coarse crumbs. Press mixture onto bottom of a 9-inch-square baking pan. Bake in preheated oven 20 to 22 minutes or until mixture begins to brown on edges. In a medium bowl, combine egg, condensed milk and vanilla until well blended. Stir in cashews, coconut and white chocolate. Spoon over hot pastry. Return to oven; bake 28 to 30 minutes or until light-golden brown. Remove from oven. Cool on a rack; cut into 1-1/2-inch bars. Makes about 36 bars.

◆

Royal Viking Almond Cookies

This idea was borrowed from the Royal Viking cruise line. We enjoyed many elaborate desserts while cruising, but this is a quick and easy one for you to feature at a fancy tea or reception.

1 (7-oz.) package almond paste
1/4 cup granulated sugar
1/4 cup sifted powdered sugar

1 egg white
Sliced almonds

Preheat oven to 350F (175C). Line 2 baking sheets with parchment paper; lightly grease the paper. Using your fingers, crumble the almond paste into a medium bowl. Add granulated sugar, powdered sugar and egg white. Using an electric mixer, beat on medium speed until smooth. Drop slightly rounded teaspoons of dough, about 2 inches apart, on prepared baking sheets. Top each cookie with 1 or 2 sliced almonds. Bake in preheated oven 10 to 12 minutes or until a light golden color. Makes 30 to 32 cookies.

Peanut Butter 'n' Jelly Ravioli Cookies

A dessert that is shaped like pasta but tastes like a cookie.

1/2 cup butter or margarine, room temperature
1 cup granulated sugar
1 egg
1 teaspoon vanilla extract
1/4 teaspoon salt
1-1/2 teaspoons baking powder

1 tablespoon milk or cream
2 cups all-purpose flour
1/4 cup peanut butter
1/4 cup grape jelly
Sifted powdered sugar

In a large bowl, beat together butter, granulated sugar and egg until fluffy. Beat in vanilla, salt, baking powder and milk. Stir in flour; blend well. Divide dough in half; form each into a flattened ball. Wrap dough in plastic wrap or a plastic bag; refrigerate 2 to 3 hours or until firm. Preheat oven to 350F (175C). Roll out 1 dough ball between 2 sheets of waxed paper to an 8- to 10-inch square. Refrigerate while preparing second ball of dough. Roll out second half of dough to an 8- to 10-inch square. With the edge of a ruler, make a slight indentation in dough every 2 inches, both vertically and horizontally to form 2-inch squares. Place 1/2 teaspoon peanut butter and 1/2 teaspoon jelly in center of each 2-inch square. Remove other rolled dough from refrigerator; peel off top sheet of waxed paper. Invert onto filled sheet of dough. Peel off second sheet of waxed paper. Gently press top layer of dough around filling. With a pastry wheel or knife, cut half way between dabs of filling, to form 2-inch squares. Press edges of each square to seal; place each about 2 inches apart on large baking sheets. Bake in preheated oven 10 to 12 minutes or until golden. Remove from oven; cool on a rack. Sprinkle with powdered sugar. Makes 16 to 20 cookies.

Satellite Sundae

*Placing a paper baking cup in a custard cup provides greater
stability while forming the chocolate shell. A 2-inch ice-cream
scoop is ideal to use when filling the chocolate shells.*

6 ounces milk chocolate

1 tablespoon vegetable oil

1-1/2 cups vanilla wafer crumbs (about 32 wafers)

1 pint vanilla or other flavor ice cream

2 tablespoons chocolate-fudge topping, optional

Cut chocolate into 1/2-inch pieces. In the top of a double boiler, heat chocolate and oil over hot water until chocolate melts. Stir in wafer crumbs. Place a paper baking cup in a 6-ounce custard cup. Spoon hot-chocolate mixture into paper cup. With the back of a spoon, press chocolate mixture over bottom and up side of cup to form a shell. Refrigerate at least 30 minutes. Repeat making 6 or 7 shells. Fill a chocolate shell with a scoop of ice cream. Top with a teaspoon of fudge topping, if desired. Place in freezer. Repeat until all shells have been filled. Freeze until firm. Serve sundaes when firm or wrap each in foil or plastic wrap. Then place in a freezer bag, seal and store in freezer until needed. Makes 6 or 7 sundaes.

Frozen Peanut-Butter Horns

Keep these on hand as a readily available small-fry treat.

12 sugar cones

1 quart vanilla or other flavor ice cream

Gently fill a sugar cone with 4 alternate layers of cold Peanut-Butter Topping and ice cream, topping cone with a 2-inch scoop of ice cream. With the back of a spoon, make a depression in scoop of ice cream; fill depression with 1 teaspoon topping. Set cone upright in a mug or juice glass; place in freezer. Continue filling remaining cones as above. Freeze filled cones 1 to 2 hours or until ice cream is firm. Serve when firm or wrap each cone in foil or plastic wrap. Place wrapped cones in a freezer bag; seal and store in freezer until needed. Makes 12 servings.

Peanut-Butter Topping:

1/4 cup granulated sugar

1/4 cup packed light brown sugar

1/2 cup evaporated milk

1/2 cup peanut butter

1/2 teaspoon vanilla extract

In a small saucepan, combine sugars and evaporated milk. Cook over medium-low heat, stirring constantly, until sugars dissolve and mixture begins to boil. Reduce heat; simmer and stir 2 minutes. Remove from heat; whisk in peanut butter and vanilla. Refrigerate until cold.

Variation
Peanut-Butter Sundae Sauce: Add an additional 1/2 cup evaporated milk and 2 tablespoons brown sugar.

Gingered-Almond Cups

Crystallized ginger blends with almonds to provide a delicate flavor.

1/2 cup butter or margarine, room temperature
1 (3-oz.) package cream cheese, room
   temperature
1 cup all-purpose flour
1 cup blanched almonds

1/2 cup sugar
1/4 cup orange juice
1/2 teaspoon grated orange peel
1 egg
1 tablespoon finely chopped crystallized ginger

In a small bowl, combine butter, cream cheese and flour. With a pastry blender or fork, blend until mixture resembles coarse crumbs. Form mixture into a ball; divide into 24 equal pieces. If difficult to handle, refrigerate 1 hour. Press each piece of pastry into a 1-3/4-inch miniature muffin cup. Make a small well in center, building up sides. Refrigerate while making filling. Preheat oven to 375F (190C). In a blender or food processor fitted with the metal blade, combine almonds, sugar and orange juice. Process until nuts are very fine. Add orange peel, egg and ginger; process until well blended. Spoon into pastry-lined muffin cups. Bake in preheated oven 20 to 30 minutes or until firm. Remove from oven; cool on a rack. Makes 24 servings.

Chocolate-Cashew Baklava Wrap-Ups

It's hard to beat a combination of chocolate and cashew nuts—especially when they're wrapped in crunchy baked filo.

1 cup sugar
3/4 cup water
1/2 teaspoon grated orange peel
1 (4-inch) cinnamon stick

1/2 cup (3 oz.) semisweet-chocolate pieces
1 cup finely chopped cashews
12 sheets filo dough
3/4 cup butter, melted

In a medium saucepan, combine sugar, water, orange peel and cinnamon stick. Bring to a boil over medium-high heat; reduce heat and simmer 12 minutes or until slightly syrupy. Remove from heat; strain to remove orange peel and cinnamon stick. While mixture is still hot, add chocolate pieces. Return to very low heat, stirring until chocolate melts; stir in cashews. Preheat oven to 400F (205C). Brush 1 side of a sheet of filo dough with butter; fold in half crosswise, with buttered sides together. Brush top of folded sheet with butter. Spoon about 2 tablespoons nut mixture to within 2 inches of short side of filo. Roll up about 3/4 of filled filo; fold in ends and finish rolling like a jelly roll. Seal edges with melted butter. Place roll, cut-side down, on a 15" x 10" jelly-roll pan. Repeat with remaining filo and filling, placing rolls about 1-inch apart in a shallow baking pan. Bake in preheated oven 12 minutes or until golden brown. Remove from oven; cool on a rack. Makes 12 servings.

Petit Brazilian Gâteau

Flavor can be varied by using almonds instead of Brazil nuts and almond liqueur in place of coffee liqueur.

1/3 cup butter or margarine, room temperature
1/2 cup lightly packed brown sugar
3 eggs, separated
2 ounces semisweet chocolate, melted
1/2 teaspoon vanilla extract

1/2 teaspoon baking powder
1/2 cup all-purpose flour
1/3 cup Brazil nuts, ground
Sifted cocoa powder for garnish
Whole or sliced Brazil nuts for garnish

Preheat oven to 350F (175C). Grease and flour 12 (3-inch) quiche pans. In a medium bowl, beat together butter and brown sugar. Add egg yolks; beat until fluffy. Stir in chocolate and vanilla. Add baking powder and flour, beating until well blended. Stir in ground nuts. In another medium bowl, beat egg whites until stiff but not dry; fold into batter. Spoon into prepared pans. Place filled pans on a 15" x 10" jellyroll pan; bake in preheated oven 13 to 15 minutes or until top springs back when lightly touched with your finger tip. Remove from oven; let stand 5 minutes. Invert each cake onto a cooling rack; cool well. Pipe or spread a thick layer of Coffee 'n' Cream Frosting over top of each cooled cake. Sprinkle lightly with sifted cocoa powder. Garnish with whole or sliced Brazil nuts. Makes 12 servings.

Coffee 'n' Cream Frosting:

1 teaspoon unflavored gelatin powder
3 tablespoons coffee liqueur
1/2 teaspoon vanilla extract

1 cup whipping cream
2 tablespoons powdered sugar

In a small saucepan, combine gelatin and liqueur. Let stand 5 minutes. Heat, stirring constantly, over low heat until gelatin dissolves. Cool until lukewarm. Stir in vanilla. In a medium bowl, whip the cream to soft peaks. Gradually add lukewarm gelatin and powdered sugar, beating until stiff peaks form.

Petit Brazilian Gâteau, above, and Raspberry-Hazelnut Stacks, page 76.

♦

Island Magic Cakes

*We prefer flaked coconut for this recipe. If you use the shredded
type, cut it into short pieces so it will be easier to get out of the pans.*

1/2 cup flaked coconut

2 tablespoons butter or margarine, melted

2 tablespoons brown sugar

1 tablespoon finely chopped crystallized ginger

1/3 cup butter or margarine, room temperature

1-1/4 cups granulated sugar

3 eggs

1/4 teaspoon almond extract

1/8 teaspoon salt

1/4 teaspoon baking soda

1-1/2 cups all-purpose flour

1/2 cup dairy sour cream

Preheat oven to 350F (175C). In a small bowl, combine coconut, melted butter, brown sugar and ginger. Lightly press coconut mixture onto bottom of 8 (3-inch) fluted pans or individual brioche pans. In a large bowl, beat 1/3 cup butter and granulated sugar until well blended. Beat in eggs, 1 at a time, until fluffy. Add almond extract, salt, baking soda and 1/2 the flour; then 1/2 the sour cream. Repeat until all is well blended. Spoon over coconut mixture in pans. Bake in preheated oven 25 to 30 minutes or until cake springs back when gently touched with your finger tip. Remove from oven. Invert cakes onto cooling racks. Cool 5 minutes; run a small spatula around edge to loosen. Makes 8 servings.

Strawberry-Meringue Swirls

*For an extra-special treat, put two swirls together with whipped
cream between.*

3 egg whites, room temperature

1/4 teaspoon cream of tartar

1 cup sugar

2 tablespoons strawberry preserves

3 drops red food coloring

Additional strawberry preserves

Preheat oven to 225F (105C). Line a baking sheet with parchment paper. In a medium bowl, beat egg whites until foamy. Add cream of tartar; beat until soft peaks form. Gradually add sugar, beating until very stiff peaks form. Add 2 tablespoons preserves and food coloring; beat 2 minutes or until very stiff. Fit a pastry bag with a large star tip; fill bag with meringue mixture. Pipe mixture into "S" shapes, about 2 inches long, on prepared baking sheet. Bake in preheated oven 1 hour. Turn oven off; let meringues cool in oven with door closed 1 to 1-1/4 hours or until thoroughly dry. Just before serving, drizzle tops with additional preserves. Makes about 32 servings.

Sicilian Chocolate-Pistachio Cannolis

*There's a hint of mocha in the shells to complement a rich
ricotta-chocolate filling. For crisp shells, fill them within an hour of
serving time.*

2 tablespoons butter or margarine, room
  temperature
1/4 cup granulated sugar
1 egg
1 tablespoon coffee-flavored liqueur

1/2 teaspoon baking powder
1/2 teaspoon unsweetened cocoa powder
1 cup all-purpose flour
5 tablespoons chopped pistachios
Powdered sugar

In a medium bowl, cream butter and granulated sugar until fluffy; beat in egg and liqueur. Stir in baking powder, cocoa powder and flour. Divide dough in half; wrap in plastic wrap or place in a plastic bag. Refrigerate dough about 1 hour. Preheat oven to 375F (190C). Lightly grease cannoli tubes. On a lightly floured board, roll out dough to a 1/16 inch thickness. Cut into 3-1/2-inch squares. Place a greased cannoli tube diagonally across center of each dough square. Slightly overlap right and left corners of dough. Pinch edges to seal. Place wrapped tubes on a baking sheet. Bake in preheated oven 10 minutes or until firm. Remove from pan; cool on a rack about 2 minutes. Carefully slide cannoli tubes out; cool completely. Spoon about 2-1/2 tablespoons Chocolate-Pistachio Filling into each cooled shell. Dip ends in chopped pistachios. Refrigerate until ready to serve. To serve, sprinkle tops with powdered sugar. Makes 12 servings.

Chocolate-Pistachio Filling:

1-1/2 cups (12 oz.) ricotta cheese
6 tablespoons powdered sugar
3/4 teaspoon vanilla extract
3/4 teaspoon grated orange peel

1/3 cup miniature semisweet-chocolate pieces
  (about 2 oz.)
3 tablespoons chopped pistachios

In a small bowl, beat together ricotta cheese, sugar and vanilla. Stir in orange peel, chocolate pieces and 3 tablespoons pistachios.

Finger-Food Buffets

Pickup foods make an impressive presentation for guests and are easy on the host or hostess. The actual set-up of a finger-food buffet requires little or no silverware. Just make sure that you have an adequate supply of napkins for the occasion. In fact, this is a good time to use attractive paper napkins with a design that is appropriate to the time of year or occasion. Count on using more than usual.

As far as food is concerned, it is exciting to serve a variety of dishes made of individual portions. Cut meats or chicken into small units; then serve them on small picks or wrap them in some kind of pastry to make it easier for guests to pick up and eat. Recipes range from Honey-Mustard Turkey Cubes served on small picks to Sesame-Crab Dumplings enclosed in won-ton wrappers.

Finger-food salads and vegetables need to be divided into individual servings and wrapped in a food that can be picked up. Roast Beef Wrap-Around Salad has a center of roast beef blended with seasonings and vegetables, then wrapped in leaf lettuce. The same principle is applied to Sicilian Prosciutto Roll-Arounds where thin strips of zucchini are marinated, then wrapped in slices of prosciutto.

Avoid last-minute panic by carefully planning a buffet menu. Include some foods that can be partially or completely made ahead.

Double Salmon Pinwheels

The exact yield depends on the size and shape of each slice of lox. Our tests are based on slices averaging 6" x 2".
(Photo on previous pages.)

6 ounces thinly sliced smoked salmon (lox)

1/4 cup dairy sour cream

1 hard-cooked egg, coarsely chopped

1 teaspoon chopped chives

1 teaspoon prepared horseradish

1 teaspoon lemon juice

1 teaspoon chopped fresh dill

Dash hot-pepper sauce

2 tablespoons butter or margarine, melted

Black caviar

Sprigs of fresh dill

Lemon peel curls

Set aside 4 slices salmon. In a small bowl, coarsely chop remaining salmon. In a food processor fitted with the metal blade, combine chopped salmon, sour cream, hard-cooked egg, chives, horseradish, lemon juice, chopped dill, hot-pepper sauce and butter. Process until mixture is almost smooth. Cut reserved salmon slices in half crosswise, forming 8 (3" x 2") pieces. Spread each piece with pureed mixture. Roll up lengthwise. Refrigerate at least 1 hour. Just before serving, cut each roll in halves or thirds. Set each on a cut end. Top with a dab of caviar, a fresh sprig of dill and a lemon-peel curl. Makes 16 to 24 servings.

Beefy-Mushroom Pinwheels

Best when eaten within an hour or two after they're made. Sliced chipped beef from the deli or in jars may be substituted.

1 tablespoon vegetable oil

1 cup (3 oz.) finely chopped mushrooms

2 tablespoons chopped watercress

1/2 of a (1.25 oz.) envelope dry onion-soup mix
   (about 3 tablespoons)

3/4 cup dairy sour cream

1 teaspoon prepared horseradish

10 thin slices spiced beef (about 2 oz.)

Sprigs of watercress for garnish

In a small skillet, heat oil. Add mushrooms; sauté over medium heat until liquid evaporates. Remove from heat. Stir in chopped watercress, dry onion-soup mix, sour cream and horseradish. Spread about 2 tablespoons mixture over each slice of meat to within 1/4 inch of edges; gently roll up. Cover and refrigerate 1 hour. Cut each roll into 4 pieces. Garnish with sprigs of watercress. Makes 40 servings.

Chicken-Mushroom Rounds

They're like little flat sandwiches with a crunchy chicken filling.

2 cups diced cooked chicken or turkey
2 tablespoons chopped green onion
1 cup small mushrooms, halved
1 garlic clove, chopped
1/2 cup chopped jicama
1/4 cup chopped red bell pepper

2 or 3 dashes hot-pepper sauce
1/4 teaspoon salt
1/8 teaspoon black pepper
24 (3-inch) round won-ton wrappers
2 tablespoons butter or margarine
2 tablespoons vegetable oil

In a food processor fitted with the metal blade, combine chicken, green onion, mushrooms, garlic, jicama, red pepper, hot-pepper sauce, salt and black pepper. Process until chopped but not pureed. Spoon about 2 tablespoons mixture onto center of 12 won-ton wrappers. Lightly brush edges with water. Top each with another won-ton wrapper; press edges to seal. In a large skillet, heat butter and oil. Place a single layer of filled won tons in hot skillet. Lightly brown one side; turn and brown other side. Repeat with remaining filled won tons. Serve warm. Makes 12 servings.

Sicilian Prosciutto Roll-Arounds

*We were so impressed with this wonderful combination of foods
while on a trip to Sicily, that we improvised our own recipe.*

2 medium zucchini
1/4 cup white-wine vinegar
3/4 cup olive oil or vegetable oil
1 garlic clove, crushed
1/4 teaspoon salt

1/8 teaspoon pepper
1 tablespoon finely chopped fresh parsley
3 ounces thinly sliced prosciutto
2-1/2 ounces string cheese or sliced mozzarella

Slice each zucchini lengthwise into approximately 8 very thin slices. Steam slices 8 to 10 minutes or until tender. In a 9-inch loaf dish, combine vinegar, oil, garlic, salt, pepper and parsley. Add zucchini slices; cover and refrigerate overnight. Cut prosciutto into 16 thin strips, approximately 6" x 1". Pull or cut string cheese into 16 thin strips. Preheat oven to 350F (175C). Drain zucchini. Place 1 zucchini slice on a slice of prosciutto. Top with a piece of cheese. Roll up prosciutto, enclosing zucchini and cheese. Secure with a small wooden pick. Place in a shallow baking pan. Bake in preheated oven 10 minutes or until cheese begins to melt. Remove from oven; serve warm or at room temperature. Makes 16 servings.

Dilly-Tuna Mousse Puffs

When brushing tops of unbaked puffs with egg glaze, be careful that glaze does not run down sides to baking pan. It will interfere with baking process, resulting in less volume.

1/2 cup water

1/4 cup butter or margarine, cut into eighths

1/4 teaspoon dry mustard

1/8 teaspoon salt

1/8 teaspoon white pepper

1/2 cup all-purpose flour

2 eggs

1-1/2 tablespoons finely chopped fresh dill

1/2 teaspoon grated lemon peel

1 egg

1 teaspoon water

Fresh dill for garnish

Preheat oven to 400F (205C). Lightly grease a large baking sheet. In a large saucepan, combine water, butter, mustard, salt and white pepper; bring to a rolling boil. Reduce heat to low. Add flour, all at once, stirring vigorously with a wooden spoon until mixture forms a thick mass and pulls away from the side of the pan. Remove from heat; let stand to cool slightly, about 5 minutes. Add eggs, 1 at a time, beating well after each addition. Beat in dill and lemon peel. For each puff, spoon about 2 tablespoons batter onto prepared baking sheet to form a 2-inch round. In a small cup, combine egg and water. Lightly brush tops with egg mixture. Bake in preheated oven 20 to 25 minutes or until puffed and golden brown. Pierce each puff with a small knife to release steam. Return to hot oven with heat off; let stand 10 minutes or until interiors are dry. Cool on a wire rack. Cut off tops, and if necessary, pull out any soft dough from inside. Spoon 2-1/2 to 3 tablespoons Tuna-Mousse Filling into each baked puff. Garnish with fresh dill. Makes 12 to 15 puffs.

Tuna-Mousse Filling:

2 teaspoons unflavored gelatin powder

2 tablespoons lemon juice

1/4 cup chopped onion

1 teaspoon grated lemon peel

1/2 cup boiling water

1/2 teaspoon salt

1/2 teaspoon dry mustard

1/8 teaspoon ground red pepper

1/4 cup dry vermouth

1/4 cup mayonnaise

1 (12-1/2-oz.) can tuna, well drained

1/3 cup whipping cream

In a small bowl, soften gelatin in lemon juice. Place in a blender or food processor fitted with the metal blade. Add onion, lemon peel and boiling water. Process until onion is pureed. Add salt, mustard, red pepper, vermouth, mayonnaise and tuna. Process 30 seconds or until well blended. With motor running, gradually add cream. Spoon into a medium bowl; cover and refrigerate until set.

Tuna-Stuffed Mushrooms

Chop the leftover mushroom stems and add to a soup or sauté them to accompany meats or chicken.

1 (6-1/2-oz.) can tuna, drained
1/4 cup soft bread crumbs
1/4 cup mayonnaise
1 tablespoon chopped green onion

1 teaspoon Worcestershire sauce
2 tablespoons grated carrot
16 to 18 mushrooms

In a food processor fitted with the metal blade, combine tuna, bread crumbs, mayonnaise, green onion and Worcestershire sauce. Process until almost smooth. Stir in carrot. Preheat oven to 375F (190C). Remove stems from mushrooms; save for another purpose. Spoon about 1 tablespoon tuna mixture into center of each mushroom. Place in a shallow baking pan. Cover with foil. Bake 10 to 15 minutes or until hot. Makes 16 to 18 stuffed mushrooms.

Bacon & Cheese Polenta Squares

An updated version of the traditional Italian polenta, cut into small squares so you can pick it up.

1 tablespoon butter or margarine
1 cup chicken stock or bouillon
1/2 cup yellow cornmeal
1 small onion, chopped
1/2 teaspoon salt
1/8 teaspoon pepper

2 slices bacon, cooked, crumbled
1 tablespoon chopped cilantro
2 eggs, beaten slightly
1/2 cup cooked whole-kernel corn
1/4 cup (1 oz.) shredded Cheddar cheese

Preheat oven to 400F (205C). Line an 8-inch-square baking pan with foil; grease foil. In a medium saucepan, bring butter and stock to a boil. Slowly pour in cornmeal, stirring constantly. Add onion, salt and pepper. Cook over medium heat 5 minutes or until thick. Remove from heat; stir in bacon, cilantro, eggs and corn. Spoon into prepared pan. Sprinkle with cheese. Bake in preheated oven 12 minutes or until cheese is bubbly. Remove from oven; let stand 5 to 10 minutes before cutting. Cut into 1-inch squares. Makes about 50 squares.

Gingered Shrimp Balls

The mixture has a tendency to stick to your fingers while forming balls. If this is a problem, chill it in the refrigerator for about an hour; then dip hands in cold water before shaping shrimp mixture.

1 pound uncooked medium shrimp, shelled
1 tablespoon grated fresh ginger
1/2 cup canned sliced water chestnuts
2 tablespoons cornstarch
1 tablespoon soy sauce

1 teaspoon sesame oil
2 tablespoons chopped green onion
1/4 cup loosely packed cilantro leaves
1 egg white
Hot mustard, optional

In a food processor fitted with the metal blade, combine shrimp, ginger, water chestnuts, cornstarch, soy sauce, sesame oil, green onion, cilantro and egg white. Process until finely chopped but not pureed. Shape into 1-1/2-inch balls. Lightly oil a heatproof plate; place balls on prepared plate. Place in top of a steamer. Pour 2 cups boiling water in bottom of steamer. Cover; steam 12 minutes or until firm. If steamer is not large enough to accommodate the entire recipe, steam 1/2 recipe at a time. Serve with hot mustard, if desired. Makes 25 to 30 meatballs.

Sesame-Crab Dumplings

Pinch tiny pleats in top of filled won-ton wrappers and you'll end up with little dumplings shaped like a vase.

7 ounces fresh, frozen or canned crabmeat
1/2 teaspoon grated fresh ginger
1 egg, beaten slightly
2 tablespoons plum sauce
2 tablespoons chopped green onion
1/4 cup chopped water chestnuts

1/4 teaspoon salt
1/8 teaspoon pepper
20 to 25 (3-inch) round won-ton wrappers
1 teaspoon toasted sesame seeds or black
    sesame seeds

In a small bowl, flake crabmeat. Blend in ginger, egg, plum sauce, green onion, water chestnuts, salt and pepper. Spoon about 2 teaspoons crab mixture onto center of each won-ton wrapper. Bring edge up around filling on all sides, pinching pleats as you go. Leave top open. Sprinkle top with toasted sesame seeds or black sesame seeds. Bring about 2 cups water to a boil in a wok or 12-inch skillet. Arrange dumplings, open-side up, on a steamer rack in wok or skillet. Cover; steam over low heat 10 to 12 minutes or until won-ton wrappers are translucent. Serve warm. Makes 20 to 25 servings.

Honey-Mustard Turkey Cubes

Packages of turkey steaks or cutlets are handy to use for this recipe.

2 tablespoons butter or margarine

1 pound uncooked turkey, cut into 1-inch pieces

2 tablespoons honey

2 tablespoons Dijon-style mustard

1 teaspoon lemon juice

1 teaspoon curry powder

1/4 teaspoon salt

1 garlic clove, crushed

Chopped chives for garnish

In a large skillet, melt butter. Add turkey; stir and cook 2 to 3 minutes or until turkey is opaque. Add honey, mustard, lemon juice, curry powder, salt and garlic. Cook and stir another 2 minutes. Sprinkle with chives. Serve hot on small picks. Makes 30 to 35 pieces.

All-American Turkey Meatballs

An updated version of ever-popular meatballs. We like it because it is lighter than the original dish. Cranberry sauce keeps it moist and flavorful.

1 pound ground turkey

1 egg, beaten slightly

1/2 cup soft bread crumbs

3/4 cup jellied cranberry sauce

1/4 cup milk

1 tablespoon finely chopped fresh parsley

1/2 teaspoon salt

1/4 cup steak sauce

1/8 teaspoon ground allspice

1 tablespoon sliced chives

1 tablespoon white wine

Preheat oven to 375F (190C). In a large bowl, combine turkey, egg, bread crumbs, 1/4 cup cranberry sauce, milk, parsley and salt. Shape mixture into 1-1/4-inch balls. Arrange balls on a broiler pan. Bake 15 to 20 minutes. Arrange in a serving dish. In a small saucepan, heat remaining 1/2 cup cranberry sauce, steak sauce and allspice until melted. Stir in chives and wine. Spoon over meatballs. Serve with small picks. Makes about 50 meatballs.

Bombay Chicken Pinwheels

*When making Dipping Sauce, be sure to finely chop all pieces of
fruit in the chutney.*

4 boneless chicken-breast halves, skinned (about
   1 lb.)

1 tablespoon Dijon-style mustard

1 tablespoon butter or margarine, melted

1/4 teaspoon salt

1/8 teaspoon pepper

2 tablespoons butter or margarine

Lightly pound chicken breasts between 2 sheets of waxed paper until about 1/4 inch thick. In a small bowl, combine mustard, 1 tablespoon butter, salt and pepper. Spread top side of pounded chicken pieces with mustard mixture. Starting with long edge, tightly roll chicken like a jelly roll. Secure with a small wooden pick. Repeat with remaining chicken. In a 10-inch skillet, melt 2 tablespoons butter. Add chicken rolls; cook over medium-low heat on all sides about 10 minutes. Remove from heat; cool. Cut each roll into 1/2-inch-thick crosswise slices. Insert a small wooden pick into each slice. Coat with Dipping Sauce. Makes about 36 pinwheels.

Dipping Sauce:

1/4 cup chutney, fruit finely chopped

1/2 cup peanut butter

1/2 cup chicken stock or bouillon

1 tablespoon honey

1/4 teaspoon crushed red-pepper flakes

1 garlic clove, crushed

In a 1-quart saucepan, combine chutney, peanut butter, stock, honey, red-pepper flakes and garlic. Bring to a boil; simmer 5 minutes.

Chicken Chunks

*A different type of sweet-sour taste that makes chicken so popular
with everyone.*

1 pound boneless chicken breasts, skinned

1/2 teaspoon salt

1/8 teaspoon pepper

1/4 cup butter or margarine

1/2 cup plum jam

2 teaspoons prepared mustard

2 teaspoons prepared horseradish

1 teaspoon lemon juice

1/8 teaspoon ground mace

Cut chicken into 1-1/2-inch pieces. Sprinkle with salt and pepper. In a 10-inch skillet, melt butter. Add chicken; sauté 5 minutes or until firm. In a small saucepan, combine plum jam, mustard, horseradish, lemon juice and mace. Heat and stir until well blended. Add cooked chicken; heat until coated with sauce. Serve with small wooden picks. Makes 30 to 35 servings.

Roast Beef Wrap-Around Salad

When wrapping lettuce around beef mixture, roll it sideways in order to end up with an attractive ruffled top.

1 cup (4 oz.) diced cold roast beef
1/4 cup dairy sour cream
1 teaspoon prepared horseradish
1/2 cup soft bread crumbs
1 tablespoon chopped green onion

1 teaspoon Dijon-style mustard
1/2 cup shredded carrot
1 teaspoon finely chopped fresh parsley
8 to 10 leaves salad bowl lettuce or leaf lettuce

In a blender or food processor fitted with the metal blade, combine roast beef, sour cream, horseradish, bread crumbs, green onion and mustard. Process until well blended. Stir in carrot and parsley. If leaves are large, cut in half through center rib. Spread about 2 tablespoons beef mixture on each leaf; roll up. Makes 8 to 10 servings.

Corned-Beef Pâté

Distinctive flavor of corned beef creates a special pâté. We enjoy the finely chopped texture instead of a smooth mixture often associated with pâté.

2 cups (10 oz.) cooked lean corned beef, cut in
   cubes
2 tablespoons finely chopped green onion
2 tablespoons finely chopped parsley
3 tablespoons finely chopped dill pickle

1/4 cup mayonnaise
2 tablespoons butter or margarine, melted
1 tablespoon coarse-grain mustard
1 teaspoon Worcestershire sauce
Rye bread or crackers

Lightly grease a 2- or 3-cup gelatin mold with vegetable oil. In a food processor fitted with the metal blade, combine corned beef, green onion, parsley and dill pickle. Process until finely chopped. Add mayonnaise, butter, mustard and Worcestershire sauce; process until blended but not smooth. Spoon into prepared mold. Cover and refrigerate at least 2 hours. Unmold onto a serving plate; serve as a spread for thinly sliced rye bread or crackers. Makes about 2 cups pâté.

Jalapeño Pickled Eggs

Red-wine vinegar gives eggs a pinkish brown color. Substitute white-wine vinegar for off-white eggs. Add more jalapeños if you enjoy very hot foods.

1 cup red-wine vinegar
1 cup water
1 teaspoon pickling spices
1 garlic clove

1 small onion, sliced
1/2 teaspoon salt
2 jalapeño peppers, quartered
6 hard-cooked eggs, peeled

In a small saucepan, combine vinegar, water, pickling spices, garlic clove, onion, salt and jalapeño peppers. Bring to a boil; simmer 2 minutes. Place hard-cooked eggs in a refrigerator dish; pour hot mixture over eggs. Cover and refrigerate at least 24 hours. Makes 6 eggs.

Mexican Pork Cubes

Pick up guacamole or salsa at the deli, or prepare your favorite recipe.

2 tablespoons vegetable oil
1 large garlic clove, pressed
1/4 teaspoon dried leaf oregano, crushed
1/2 teaspoon ground cumin
1/2 teaspoon salt

1/2 teaspoon pepper
1/2 teaspoon grated orange peel
1 tablespoon orange juice
1 pound boneless pork, cut into 1-1/2-inch cubes
Guacamole or salsa for dipping

In a medium bowl, combine vegetable oil, garlic, oregano, cumin, salt, pepper, orange peel and orange juice; blend well. Add pork cubes, turning to coat evenly with mixture. Let stand at room temperature 1 hour or refrigerate 3 to 4 hours to marinate. Remove pork cubes from marinade; place on a baking sheet. Broil 4 to 5 inches from heat source 3 minutes; turn cubes. Broil another 3 minutes or until lightly browned and meat is no longer pink when slashed. Transfer pork to a heated platter. Serve hot on small wooden picks with guacamole or salsa for dipping. Makes 18 to 20 pieces.

Neapolitan Slices

Borrowed from Italy, but is equally popular throughout other parts of the world.

1 (1-lb.) loaf unsliced Italian or French bread
1 cup (8 oz.) ricotta cheese
1/4 cup chopped sun-dried tomatoes in oil
1/4 cup (3/4 oz.) grated Parmesan cheese
2 tablespoons chopped fresh basil

1/8 teaspoon pepper
4 slices mozzarella cheese (about 4 ounces)
1/4 pound thinly sliced prosciutto, chopped
2 tablespoons sliced green onion

Slice off top of bread about 1/2 inch from top, Scoop out center, leaving about 1/2 inch around sides and bottom. Save bread crumbs for another purpose. In a small bowl, combine ricotta cheese, tomatoes, Parmesan cheese, basil and pepper. Spread 1/2 mixture on bottom of scooped-out bread. Top with mozzarella cheese. Sprinkle with half the chopped prosciutto. Top with remaining ricotta mixture. Then remaining prosciutto and green onion. Top with lid of bread; refrigerate at least 2 hours. Cut crosswise into 1- to 1-1/2-inch slices. Makes 10 to 12 servings.

Maylasian Triangles

Refrigerator crescent rolls may be separated into triangles by cutting along perforations in dough. Then, with a sharp knife, cut each triangle in half to make a practical size for finger food.

4 boneless chicken-breast halves, skinned (about
   1 lb.)
1/4 cup coarsely chopped cashews
1/4 cup chutney
1/4 cup chopped green onions
1 teaspoon grated fresh ginger
1 garlic clove, crushed

1/4 cup mayonnaise
1 egg
1/2 teaspoon salt
1/8 teaspoon pepper
1 (8-oz.) package refrigerator crescent rolls
Half or whole cashews for garnish

Preheat oven to 375F (190C). Cut chicken in small pieces. In a food processor fitted with the metal blade, combine chicken, chopped cashews, chutney, green onions, ginger, garlic, mayonnaise, egg, salt and pepper. Process until finely chopped but not pureed; set aside. Unroll crescent rolls; cut each triangle in half to form 16 triangles. Arrange triangles on a baking sheet. Spread 2 to 3 tablespoons chicken mixture on top of each triangle. Bake in preheated oven 15 minutes. Garnish with half or whole cashews. Serve warm. Makes 16 servings.

Parmesan Goat-Cheese Potato Wedges

*A new twist to the classic baked potato with cheese. It's slightly
messy to pick up with your fingers—but well worth the effort.*

1/2 cup (1-1/2 oz.) grated Parmesan cheese
1/4 cup (1 oz.) crumbled goat cheese
2 tablespoons finely chopped green onion
1/4 teaspoon salt

1/8 teaspoon pepper
1 tablespoon finely chopped fresh parsley
4 large baking potatoes
1/4 cup butter or margarine, melted

Preheat oven to 400F (205C). Grease a 15" x 10" jelly-roll pan; set aside. In a small bowl, combine Parmesan cheese, goat cheese, green onion, salt, pepper and parsley. Cut each unpeeled potato lengthwise into 6 wedges. Brush cut sides of potato wedges with butter. Gently press cheese mixture over butter. Place potatoes, skin-side down, in baking pan. Bake in preheated oven 20 to 25 minutes or until tender. Makes 24 wedges.

Filo-Asparagus Fingers

Bake these seam-side up to keep cheese from oozing out.

4 sheets filo dough
1/3 cup butter or margarine, melted
2 tablespoons sweet-hot mustard

1/4 teaspoon paprika
16 spears asparagus, cooked
2 oz. Brie cheese, cut into 16 small strips

Preheat oven to 400F (205C). Cut long side of each sheet of filo into 4 lengthwise pieces, resulting in 16 strips about 14" x 4-1/2". In a small bowl, combine butter, mustard and paprika; brush on top side of filo. Place 1 cooked asparagus spear and a strip of Brie on each strip of filo. Roll up into a finger shape; place seam-side up in a shallow baking pan. Bake in preheated oven 6 to 8 minutes or until filo is golden brown. Serve immediately. Makes 16 servings.

Glazed Carrot Rolls

Use thinly sliced ham so it can be wrapped tightly around carrots.

2 large carrots, peeled
1 tablespoon butter or margarine
3 tablespoons brown sugar

10 (4-inch-square) thin ham slices
Ground mace

Cut each carrot into 8 lengthwise sticks; then in half crosswise. Cook carrot sticks in boiling water until barely tender; drain. In a medium skillet, melt butter and brown sugar. Add cooked carrots; cook and stir over medium-low heat 2 minutes. Refrigerate carrots in butter-sugar glaze at least 2 hours. Place 3 cooled, glazed carrot sticks on each slice of ham. Sprinkle with a dash of ground mace; roll up. Makes 10 servings.

Round-the-Clock Snacks

Everyone loves snacks. Sports fans who arrange their weekends around the televised game schedule munch on everything from bags of peanuts to elaborate multi-layered sandwiches. Those attending sports events start snacking at the ever-popular tailgate parties, and continue with a wide variety of goodies from the stadium snack bar. Movie fans consider a jumbo container of popcorn and a soft drink as essential as an admission ticket to the theater. The waiting line at a frozen-yogurt or ice-cream store on a hot summer evening is evidence that all ages are avid snackers.

At home, snacks are popular throughout the day. As soon as children get home from school, the question is, "What's to eat?" Our S'Mores Bars, made with the traditional graham crackers, chocolate, and marshmallows, are done easily in your oven, but bring fond memories of camping trips. Sunset Pops, made in small paper cups, have alternate layers of orange sherbet and vanilla ice cream studded with mini-pieces of candy orange slices.

For popcorn fans, we offer magical combinations that range from spicy seasonings to Hawaiian flavors. If these ideas don't appeal to you, we've added licorice bits to popcorn balls and chocolate and peanuts to popcorn clusters.

Sunset Pops

*We suggest using 3-ounce paper cups for small-fry servings and
5-ounce cups for those with more aggressive appetites.
(Photo on previous pages.)*

4 ounces (about 6) candy orange slices
1 pint vanilla ice cream

1 pint orange sherbet

With kitchen shears, cut orange slices into pea-sized pieces. Separate pieces as much as possible. Soften vanilla ice cream slightly; stir in candy pieces until they are well distributed. Spoon 4 alternate layers of orange sherbet and vanilla ice cream into a paper cup. Insert a wooden ice-cream stick in center of cup; place in freezer. Continue until all cups are filled. When pops are firm, about 1 to 2 hours, tear off paper cups. Serve immediately or wrap each pop in foil or plastic wrap and place in a freezer bag. Seal and store in freezer until needed. Makes 6 (5-oz.) or 10 (3-oz.) pops.

Butterscotch-Macaroon Ice-Cream Sandwich

A make-ahead treat that can be kept in the freezer several weeks.

24 (2-1/2-inch) crisp macaroon cookies
1 pint vanilla or other ice cream, slightly softened

Spread 1 tablespoon cold Butterscotch-Almond Topping on the flat side of a cookie; then spread 1 rounded tablespoon ice cream on flat side of another cookie. Press the 2 cookies together forming a sandwich. Place in freezer immediately. Continue until 12 sandwiches are made. Serve when sandwich fillings are firm, or wrap each sandwich in foil or plastic wrap and place in a freezer bag. Seal and store in freezer until needed. Makes 12 cookie sandwiches.

Butterscotch-Almond Topping:

**1 (6-oz.) package butterscotch pieces (about 1
   cup)**
2 teaspoons butter or margarine

2 tablespoons evaporated milk
3 ounces toasted almonds, chopped

In the top of a double boiler over hot water, heat butterscotch pieces, butter and evaporated milk until blended. Remove from heat; stir in chopped almonds. Refrigerate until cold.

Variation
Butterscotch-Almond Sundae Sauce: Add an additional 1/3 cup evaporated milk to the above topping recipe.

S'Mores Bars

A home-style version of the favorite combination usually associated with campfire cooking.

1-1/2 cups graham-cracker crumbs (about 17 graham-cracker squares)
1/4 cup lightly packed brown sugar
1/2 cup butter or margarine

1 cup miniature marshmallows
1 (6-oz.) package milk-chocolate pieces (about 1 cup)

Preheat oven to 350F (175C). In a medium bowl, combine graham-cracker crumbs, brown sugar and butter. With a pastry blender or a fork, blend until mixture resembles coarse crumbs. Press mixture on bottom of a 9-inch-square or round baking pan. Bake in preheated oven 12 to 15 minutes or until edges begin to brown. Remove from oven. Immediately sprinkle top with marshmallows and chocolate pieces. Return to oven 5 minutes or until marshmallows puff. Remove from oven; cool on a rack. Cut into 1-1/2- or 1-3/4-inch squares. Makes 20 to 25 bars.

Cream & Sugar-Stuffed Strawberries

At their very best when eaten right away. A very impressive addition to a fruit tray or dessert buffet. (Photo on page 79.)

1/4 cup (2 oz.) Neufchâtel cheese, room temperature
2 tablespoons dairy sour cream

12 to 14 large strawberries
2 tablespoons brown sugar

In a small bowl, combine cheese and sour cream. Make an "X" cut in each strawberry from pointed end almost to stem, being careful to keep each berry in 1 piece. Carefully open berries as much as possible. Pipe or spoon in cheese mixture. Sprinkle brown sugar on top. Serve within 1 hour. Makes 12 to 14 stuffed strawberries.

Orange-Spiced Nuts

Spicy coating with a touch of orange is a complementary flavor for nuts. Package them in an attractive container for an ideal gift.

1/2 cup sugar
1/2 teaspoon ground cinnamon
1/4 teaspoon ground nutmeg
1/4 teaspoon ground cardamom

1 egg white
1 tablespoon orange juice
1/4 teaspoon grated orange peel
2 cups walnut or pecan halves

Preheat oven to 250F (120C). Line a baking sheet with parchment paper; lightly grease paper. In a medium bowl, combine sugar, cinnamon, nutmeg and cardamom. In another medium bowl, combine egg white, orange juice and orange peel; beat slightly. Dip walnuts or pecans in egg-white mixture, then in sugar mixture. Place on prepared baking sheet; do not let them touch. Sprinkle any remaining sugar mixture over nuts. Bake in preheated oven 1 hour. Makes 2-1/2 to 3 cups.

Ginger-Almond Balls

A no-bake treat that's a cross between a confection and a cookie. Refrigerate for a firm texture.

20 to 25 crisp coconut macaroons, coarsely broken
1/2 cup toasted slivered almonds
1/4 cup candied orange peel

1 tablespoon chopped crystallized ginger
1/2 cup powdered sugar
1/3 cup orange juice
1 cup toasted slivered almonds, coarsely chopped

In a food processor fitted with the metal blade, combine macaroons, 1/2 cup almonds, candied orange peel, ginger, powdered sugar and orange juice. Process until finely chopped. Shape into 1-1/2-inch balls. Roll in coarsely chopped almonds. Makes 35 to 40 balls.

Spiced Fruit & Nut Clusters

Use one kind of nut or your favorite combination. We like to use a can of mixed nuts so we can sample a variety.

1/2 cup orange juice
1-1/2 cups sugar
1/4 teaspoon ground cinnamon
1/4 teaspoon ground mace

1/4 teaspoon grated orange peel
1 (6-oz.) package dried fruit morsels (1-1/2 cups),
   page 20
1 cup mixed shelled nuts

In a 3-quart saucepan, bring orange juice and sugar to a boil. Cook mixture to 238F (110C) or the soft-ball stage when dropped into cold water. Remove from heat. Add cinnamon, mace, orange peel, dried fruit morsels and nuts. Stir until syrup begins to look cloudy. Before mixture hardens, pour onto a 15" x 10" jelly-roll pan; use a rubber spatula to spread mixture. Using 2 forks, pull mixture apart into small clusters. Makes about 6 cups.

Chocolate-Almond Truffles

Super wonderful and super rich! Keep in the refrigerator until serving time.

8 ounces semisweet chocolate, coarsely
   chopped
1/2 cup whipping cream

1 tablespoon butter
1 tablespoon almond liqueur
2/3 cup finely chopped toasted almonds

Melt chocolate in a double boiler over hot water or in a microwave-proof container; set aside. In a 1-quart saucepan, heat whipping cream and butter until melted but not boiling. Using an electric mixer, beat hot cream mixture into melted chocolate; add liqueur. Cover and refrigerate about 1-1/2 hours or until easy to handle. Pinch off about 1 tablespoon chocolate mixture. With your fingers, roll it into a 1-inch ball. Roll in chopped almonds. Repeat with remaining mixture and nuts. Refrigerate truffles until serving time. Serve on a small tray or in individual paper candy cups. Makes 18 to 20 truffles.

Bits-of-Licorice Popcorn Balls

*Chewy and crunchy, these are the ultimate snack for
all licorice lovers.*

8 cups popped popcorn

1 cup licorice bits

1 cup sugar

1/3 cup light corn syrup

1/3 cup water

1/4 cup butter or margarine

1 teaspoon anise extract

In a large bowl, combine popcorn and licorice bits. In a medium saucepan, combine sugar, corn syrup, water and butter, stirring until sugar is dissolved. Cook until mixture reaches 250F (120C) or the hard-ball stage when dropped into cold water. Remove from heat; stir in anise extract. Pour hot mixture over popcorn and licorice, tossing until well coated. With hands, form into 2-1/2- to 3-inch balls. Makes about 12 balls.

Hawaiian Popcorn

*Fond memories of Hawaii provided the inspiration for this popular
combination of ingredients.*

1/4 cup butter or margarine, melted

1 tablespoon grated fresh ginger

1 tablespoon soy sauce

1/4 teaspoon ground coriander

8 to 10 cups popped popcorn

1 cup coconut chips

1/2 cup macadamia-nut halves or broken pieces

Preheat oven to 325F (165C). In a small bowl, combine butter, ginger, soy sauce and coriander. In a large bowl, combine popcorn, coconut chips and nuts. Pour butter mixture over popcorn, tossing until well coated. Spread coated popcorn evenly on a 15" x 10" jelly-roll pan. Bake in preheated oven 10 to 12 minutes, stirring at least once. Makes about 6 cups.

Clockwise from bottom, Bits-of-Licorice Popcorn Balls, above; Peanutty-Chocolate Popcorn Clusters, page 114; and Hawaiian Popcorn, above.

Peanutty-Chocolate Popcorn Clusters

*For all chocoholics! An irresistible snack of popcorn with a
chocolate coating. (Photo on previous page.)*

8 cups popped popcorn

1 cup salted peanuts

1-1/4 cups sugar

1/3 cup light corn syrup

3/4 cup water

3 ounces semisweet chocolate

3 tablespoons butter or margarine

Grease a 15" x 10" jelly-roll pan. In a large bowl, combine popcorn and peanuts. In a 1-quart saucepan, combine sugar, corn syrup and water. Bring to a boil; cook, without stirring, until mixture reaches 242F (115C) or the firm-ball stage when dropped into cold water. In a small saucepan, melt chocolate and butter over low heat. Stir into sugar syrup after it is cooked. Pour combined syrup mixture over popcorn and nuts, tossing until well coated. Pour coated popcorn onto prepared pan, spreading it out with 2 forks. Cool 10 minutes; separate into clusters. Makes 11 to 12 cups.

Peppy Popcorn

*Popcorn shrinks slightly when heated with other ingredients, so
the volume will be slightly less than you expect.*

1/4 cup butter or margarine, melted

1 teaspoon chili powder

1/2 teaspoon seasoned pepper

1/4 teaspoon garlic salt

2 teaspoons Worcestershire sauce

8 cups popped popcorn

Preheat oven to 325F (165C). In a small bowl, combine butter, chili powder, seasoned pepper, garlic salt and Worcestershire sauce. Place popcorn in a large bowl. Pour butter mixture over popcorn; toss until well coated. Spread coated popcorn evenly on a 15" x 10" jelly-roll pan. Bake in preheated oven 10 minutes. Serve warm. Makes about 5-1/2 cups.

Granola Snack Rounds

We like to use dried fruit morsels that are cut up and ready to eat.
If you have a special favorite, such as dried apples or apricots,
use one kind.

1/4 cup butter or margarine, room temperature
1/4 cup lightly packed brown sugar
1/4 cup chunky peanut butter
1/4 cup honey
1/4 teaspoon baking soda

1/2 cup all-purpose flour
1 egg, beaten slightly
1-1/2 cups granola-type cereal
3/4 cup dried fruit morsels, page 20

Preheat oven to 350F (175C). Grease 12 (2-1/2- to 3-inch) muffin cups. In a large bowl, combine butter, brown sugar, peanut butter, honey, baking soda and flour; beat until smooth. Stir in egg, granola-type cereal and dried fruit morsels. Spoon mixture into prepared muffin cups. Bake about 15 minutes. Remove from oven; cool completely. Remove from muffin cups. Makes 12 servings.

South-of-the-Border Churros

Traditional light-textured Mexican treat in the form of a long ribbon.
For variety, make "S" or "U" shapes.

1/4 cup butter or margarine
1/2 cup water
1 teaspoon sugar
1/2 cup all-purpose flour
2 eggs

1/2 teaspoon vanilla extract
Oil for deep-frying
2 tablespoons sugar
1/2 teaspoon ground cinnamon

In a medium saucepan, combine butter, water and 1 teaspoon sugar. Bring to a full boil over medium-high heat; add flour all at once. Remove from heat; beat with a spoon until mixture forms a thick paste that leaves side of pan. Add eggs; beat until smooth and shiny. Stir in vanilla. Pour oil to a 2-inch depth in a deep-fryer or large saucepan. Heat oil to 375F (190C) or until a 1-inch bread cube turns golden brown in 50 seconds. Fit a pastry bag with a large star tip; fill bag with batter. Squeeze batter into hot oil, forming 4-inch ribbons or circles of dough. Fry until golden brown; drain on paper towels. In a small bowl, combine 2 tablespoons sugar and cinnamon. Sprinkle on hot churros. Repeat with remaining batter. Serve warm. Makes about 20 churros.

Won-Ton Treats

*Make up a quick and easy batch of walnut or date filling, or just
use about 1 teaspoon almond paste right from the package. A
larger amount of oil in the pan results in a more crisp won ton.*

Walnut Filling, Date Filling or 1/2 cup almond
   paste
16 (3-inch) round won-ton wrappers

1 egg, beaten slightly
2 to 4 tablespoons vegetable oil
2 tablespoons powdered sugar

Spoon 1 rounded teaspoon filling in center of each won-ton wrapper. Brush egg around edge of each wrapper. Fold in half; lightly press edges together to seal. With finger tips, slightly flatten filling. Heat 2 tablespoons oil in an 8-inch skillet over medium heat. Fry won tons on each side until golden brown. Drain on paper towels. Dust with powdered sugar. Makes 16 won tons.

Walnut Filling:

1/2 cup finely chopped walnuts
2 tablespoons honey

1/8 teaspoon grated lemon peel

In a small bowl, combine walnuts, honey and lemon peel.

Date Filling:

1/2 cup finely chopped dates
2 tablespoons brown sugar

3 tablespoons water

In a small saucepan, combine dates, brown sugar and water. Cook and stir 5 minutes or until texture of paste. Cool.

Ranch 'n' Surf Munchies

*Do not reconstitute salad dressing mix. The dry ingredients coat
the crackers to give them a spicy flavor that's just the right
accompaniment to cold drinks.*

2 cups small oyster crackers (1 inch diameter)
2 cups pretzel goldfish-shaped crackers
   (1 inch long)
1/2 cup roasted shelled peanuts

1 (.4-oz.) package original ranch-style salad
   dressing mix
1/2 teaspoon ground mustard
2 tablespoons vegetable oil

Mix dry ingredients in a strong plastic bag. Add oil; close opening. Shake vigorously with both hands. Makes 4-1/2 cups.

Quick Cookie Puffs

Puffy topping on sugar cookies makes them special enough for important events.

3 egg whites, room temperature
1/4 teaspoon cream of tartar
1/2 cup lightly packed brown sugar
3/4 cup finely chopped dates

1/3 cup finely chopped Brazil nuts
1/4 cup finely chopped candied orange peel
1 (20-oz.) package refrigerator sugar-cookie
   dough

Preheat oven to 375F (190C). In a medium bowl, beat egg whites and cream of tartar until foamy. Gradually add sugar, beating until stiff peaks form. Fold in dates, Brazil nuts and orange peel. Cut cookie dough into 1/4-inch-thick slices. Place on ungreased baking sheets. Spread about 1 tablespoon egg-white mixture on center of each cookie. Bake in preheated oven 10 minutes. Remove from oven; cool on a rack. Makes about 36 cookies.

Short-Cut Soft Pretzels

Alone, they're a great snack or lunch box treat. Spread them with cream cheese or soft processed cheese as a substitute for a sandwich.

1 (11-oz.) package refrigerated soft bread sticks
1 egg yolk
1 tablespoon water

Kosher salt
Sesame or caraway seeds

Separate refrigerated dough at perforations to form 8 equal pieces. Unroll each; with palms of your hands, roll each into an 18-inch-long rope. Shape each rope into a pretzel by laying in a U-shape with ends pointing away from you. About 1 inch from the ends, twist rope ends around each other at least once. Bring twisted ends down and place on top of closed end of U. Pinch ends into closed portion to seal. Pour water into a 4-quart saucepan to about 3-inch depth. Bring to a simmer. Using a slotted spoon, lower pretzels, 2 or 3 at a time, into simmering water. Cook about 20 seconds on each side. Remove from water; drain on a cooling rack. Preheat oven to 375F (190C). Lightly grease a 17" x 11" baking sheet. Arrange drained pretzels on prepared baking sheet. In a small bowl, beat egg yolk with water; brush over pretzels. Sprinkle with Kosher salt; then with sesame or caraway seeds. Bake 17 to 20 minutes or until golden brown. Makes 8 large soft pretzels.

Italian-Style Bagels

*One of our favorite ways to serve bagels. Make up the spread
ahead of time so you can produce the final dish at the last minute.*

1/4 pound pepperoni, diced

1/4 pound mozzarella cheese, diced

1/3 cup plain yogurt

1 tablespoon coarse-grain mustard

1 teaspoon chopped chives

4 bagels, split

In a blender or food processor fitted with the metal blade, combine pepperoni, mozzarella, yogurt, mustard and chives. Process until well mixed but not smooth. Spread on cut sides of bagels. Broil 4 to 5 inches from heat source 2 to 3 minutes or until bubbly. Serve warm. Makes 8 bagel halves.

Doodle Bread

*Make your favorite doodle designs by moving the funnel of batter
over hot oil in deep-fryer.*

Oil for deep-frying

1 egg

2/3 cup milk

1-1/4 cups all-purpose flour

2 tablespoons granulated sugar

1/4 teaspoon ground cinnamon

1 teaspoon baking soda

1/8 teaspoon salt

Sifted powdered sugar or honey

Pour oil to a 2-inch depth in a deep-fryer or large saucepan. Heat oil to 375F (190C) or until a 1-inch bread cube turns golden brown in 50 seconds. In a medium bowl, beat together egg, milk, flour, sugar, cinnamon, baking soda and salt. Hold finger over end of a small funnel with a 3/8-inch spout opening. Pour about half the batter in the funnel. Hold funnel over hot oil; release finger. As batter flows into oil, move funnel back and forth to form desired doodle. Fry until brown on one side; turn and brown other side. Drain well on paper towels. Sprinkle with powdered sugar or drizzle with honey. Repeat with remaining batter. Best when served right away. Makes 6 to 8 servings.

Cajun-Spiced Cracker Bread

A spicy snack that you can eat warm or at room temperature. Just break off the amount you want to eat; save the remainder for another day.

3 to 3-1/4 cups all-purpose flour
1 teaspoon sugar
1 teaspoon salt
1 (1/4-oz.) package active dry yeast (about 1 tablespoon)

1 cup very warm water (125F/50C)
1/4 cup butter or margarine, cut in small cubes, room temperature
2 tablespoons vegetable oil

In a large mixer bowl, combine 1 cup flour, sugar, salt and undissolved yeast; add warm water and butter. Using an electric mixer, beat on medium speed 2 minutes. Add 3/4 cup flour; beat on high speed 2 minutes or until stretchy. Stir in enough remaining flour, about 1-1/4 cups, to make a stiff dough. Turn out dough on a lightly floured board. Knead dough 5 to 8 minutes or until smooth and elastic. Clean and grease bowl; place dough in greased bowl, turning to grease all sides. Cover and let rise in warm place until doubled in bulk, about 45 minutes. Punch down dough; divide dough into 6 pieces. Cover and let rest 10 minutes. Preheat oven to 400F (205C). Lightly grease a large baking sheet. Roll out one piece of dough to a 12-inch circle. Carefully transfer to prepared baking sheet. Prick with a fork in several places. Brush generously with oil. Sprinkle with 3/8 teaspoon Cajun Spice mixture. Bake in preheated oven 8 minutes or until golden brown. Repeat until all dough circles are baked. Makes 6 cracker breads.

Cajun Spice:

1/4 teaspoon ground red pepper
1/4 teaspoon ground white pepper
1/4 teaspoon ground black pepper
1/4 teaspoon filé powder
1/4 teaspoon ground thyme

1/4 teaspoon paprika
1/4 teaspoon garlic powder
1/4 teaspoon onion powder
1/4 teaspoon fennel seeds
1/4 teaspoon salt

In a small bowl, combine spices.

Outdoor Finger-Food Feasts

When the weather is right for outdoor eating, everyone is interested in a table under a big shade tree at the park or a smooth spot on a sun-drenched sandy beach. The more relaxed atmosphere encourages more casual dining, with emphasis on pickup foods.

Picnics

The most important rule in planning a picnic is to keep foods cold. This means that portable coolers should be well-stocked with ice to assure well-chilled salads and desserts.

We like walk-away salads for picnics. They provide a way to encourage salad-shy grown-ups as well as children to enjoy vegetables. Everyone is more likely to pick up our Green 'n' Gold Walk-Away Salad than to try a traditional salad. Although we enjoy iceberg lettuce, we like to vary salads with leaf lettuce and what is often called "salad bowl." Both of these varieties have bright curly leaves that create a natural wrap-around for salads. Pickup salads are not always wrapped in lettuce. Deli-Potato-Salad Wrap-Ups are filled with a wonderful potato salad that's rolled inside thin slices of cold meat. Either fill them at home or take ingredients to the picnic for everyone to assemble their own. If you're looking for an unusual salad for a picnic or barbecue, try Stuffed Rice & Bean Salad. You can make it ahead, right up to the last step. Keep everything cold; then roll it in lettuce leaves while the burgers grill. Then you're ready to eat!

Barbecues

Thoughts of barbecuing bring a variety of images. It may be a barbecue grill in the backyard, a hibachi at the beach or a camp stove at a remote campsite. It brings the excitement of cooking and eating outside.

With this goes a more casual, easy way of life. Traditional silverware is often replaced with plastic utensils or with fingers. Menus are designed to fit outdoor dining. Barbecued ribs, fish and chicken top the list of favorites.

Barbecued Porkburgers with Papaya Relish

Lean ground pork is a welcome change from the traditional beef burger. Papaya relish tops it off with a fresh-fruit flavor. (Photo on previous pages.)

1-1/4 to 1-1/2 pounds lean ground pork
1 egg, beaten slightly
1 (8-oz.) can water chestnuts, drained, finely chopped
1/4 cup soft bread crumbs

1 tablespoon soy sauce
1/8 teaspoon pepper
6 pieces leaf lettuce
6 sesame-seed hamburger buns

In a medium bowl, combine pork, egg, water chestnuts, bread crumbs, soy sauce and pepper. Shape into 6 (5-inch) patties. Place patties on a barbecue grill 4 to 5 inches from heat. Cook 8 to 10 minutes on one side; turn and cook other side 7 minutes or until done. Remove from heat. Place a leaf of lettuce on bottom portion of each bun; top each with a cooked burger. With a slotted spoon, top burgers with Fresh-Papaya Relish. Place top portion of bun on top. Garnish as desired. Makes 6 servings.

Fresh-Papaya Relish:

1 small papaya, peeled, seeded, chopped
1 jalapeño pepper, seeded, chopped
1/4 cup orange juice
1 tablespoon finely chopped green onion

1 teaspoon finely chopped cilantro
1/8 teaspoon salt

At least 4 hours before serving time, in a small bowl, combine papaya, jalapeño pepper, orange juice, green onion, cilantro and salt. Cover and refrigerate.

Apricot-Pineapple Barbecued Ribs

It's almost a sweet-sour taste, combined with the more traditional smoky barbecue flavor of ribs. The bottled barbecue sauce saves preparation time and blends well with ribs.

4 pounds pork spareribs
1 (8-oz.) can crushed pineapple with juice
1/4 cup apricot preserves
3/4 cup bottled smoky barbecue sauce

1 tablespoon prepared mustard
1 small onion, chopped
1/2 teaspoon salt
1/8 teaspoon pepper

Preheat oven to 350F (175C). Cut meat into individual ribs. Place on a rack in a 15" x 10" jelly-roll pan. Cover with foil. Bake in preheated oven 50 minutes or until almost done. In a medium saucepan, combine pineapple with juice, apricot preserves, barbecue sauce, mustard, onion, salt and pepper. Simmer 10 minutes, stirring occasionally. To serve, coat each partially cooked rib with sauce. With tongs, place coated ribs on a hot grill 4 to 5 inches from heat source. Cook until brown on one side; turn and brush with sauce. Brown other side. Spoon extra sauce over meat; serve warm. Makes 15 to 18 ribs.

◆

Shangri-La Drumsticks

*To prepare these exotic drumsticks for a picnic, cook them at least
four hours before serving time. Thoroughly chill them in the
refrigerator and keep them cold en route to the picnic.
(Photo on page 129.)*

1/2 cup plain yogurt
1/2 teaspoon curry powder
1/4 teaspoon ground cumin
1 garlic clove, crushed
1 tablespoon lemon juice
1/4 teaspoon salt

1/8 teaspoon ground red pepper
1/2 cup fine dry bread crumbs
2 tablespoons sesame seeds
1 tablespoon butter or margarine, melted
8 or 9 chicken drumsticks

Preheat oven to 375F (190C). In a shallow, medium bowl, combine yogurt, curry powder, cumin, garlic, lemon juice, salt and ground red pepper. In a shallow, small bowl, combine bread crumbs and sesame seeds. Pour melted butter into a shallow baking pan. Dip chicken drumsticks into yogurt mixture; then in bread-crumb mixture. Place coated chicken in buttered pan. Bake in preheated oven 30 minutes; turn drumsticks over. Continue baking 20 minutes or until golden brown. Serve warm or refrigerate until serving time. Makes 8 or 9 drumsticks.

Mediterranean Barbecued Burgers

*These are hearty burgers, designed to fit on large oval French or
Italian rolls. For smaller servings, shape meat into five or six
patties and serve on hamburger buns.*

1-1/4 to 1-1/2 pounds lean ground beef
1 teaspoon chopped fresh oregano or 1/4
    teaspoon dried leaf oregano, crushed
1/2 teaspoon salt
1/8 teaspoon pepper
1 garlic clove, crushed

1 tablespoon chopped fresh parsley
8 pimento-stuffed green olives, sliced
4 slices mozzarella cheese
1 large tomato, cut into 4 slices
4 (5-inch) Italian or French rolls, split

In a medium bowl, combine beef, oregano, salt, pepper, garlic and parsley. Shape into 4 oval patties about 7" x 3-1/2". Place patties on a barbecue grill 4 to 5 inches from heat. Cook 5 minutes on one side; turn and cook other side 5 minutes or until almost done. Arrange 2 sliced olives on top of each; then 1 slice cheese. Heat until cheese melts. Remove from heat; place on Italian or French rolls. Top each with a tomato slice. Makes 4 servings.

◆

Barbecued Shrimp & Pepper Kabobs

To avoid overcooking, use a moderately hot barbecue and place kabobs 4 to 5 inches from heat. Chunks of zucchini or mushrooms can be substituted for bell pepper.

16 large uncooked shrimp (about 1 pound)
2 tablespoons soy sauce
2 tablespoons lemon juice
1 garlic clove, crushed
1/8 teaspoon black pepper

2 tablespoons dry white wine
2 teaspoons grated fresh ginger
2 tablespoons vegetable oil
1 large red or green bell pepper, cut into 1-inch pieces

Shell shrimp, leaving tails on. Slit shrimp lengthwise along vein, but not completely through; remove vein. In a medium bowl, combine soy sauce, lemon juice, garlic, black pepper, wine, ginger and oil. Add shrimp; cover and refrigerate at least 1 hour. On each of 4 (10- to 12-inch) skewers, thread 4 shrimp alternately with bell-pepper pieces. Brush with marinade. Place on a moderately hot barbecue grill 4 to 5 inches from heat. Cook 2 to 3 minutes. Turn and brush with sauce. Cook another 2 to 3 minutes or until done. Makes 4 servings.

Herb-Grilled Chicken

A welcome change from traditional barbecued chicken. Fresh herbs combine with mustard in a light marinade that brings out the best in the chicken.

3 pounds frying-chicken pieces
1/4 cup vegetable oil
2 tablespoons lemon juice
2 tablespoons dry white wine
1 tablespoon finely chopped fresh rosemary

1 teaspoon finely chopped fresh thyme
2 tablespoons sweet-hot mustard
1 teaspoon salt
1/4 teaspoon pepper

Arrange chicken pieces in a single layer in a large shallow baking dish. In a small bowl, combine oil, lemon juice, wine, rosemary, thyme, mustard, salt and pepper; pour mixture over chicken. Cover and refrigerate at least 4 hours or overnight, turning chicken pieces once. Remove chicken from marinade. Place on a hot barbecue grill about 4 inches from heat. Cook 30 to 40 minutes, turning frequently. Brush with reserved marinade several times during cooking. Cook chicken until juices run clear when pierced with a fork. Makes 4 to 5 servings.

Hot Bologna-Cheese Buns

Prepare them ahead of time; wrap in foil and heat on a barbecue at the park or in your backyard. Children enjoy making their own.

2 tablespoons butter or margarine, room temperature
1 teaspoon prepared or spicy mustard
4 hot-dog buns

4 (5" x 1/2") sticks Swiss or Cheddar cheese
4 slices bologna or salami
1 medium tomato, chopped

In a small bowl, combine butter and mustard. Spread on both sides of buns. Place 1 cheese stick in center of each slice of bologna or salami. Sprinkle each with chopped tomato. Roll up each slice and place in a buttered bun. Cover with lid of bun. Wrap individually in heavy-duty foil. Place foil packages on outside edge of hot barbecue grill 10 to 20 minutes or until hot. Turn at least one time. Makes 4 servings.

Skewered Szechuan-Style Barbecued Pork

If you use bamboo skewers, soak them in water several hours ahead of time to keep them from burning. (Photo on cover.)

1 pound pork tenderloin
36 (2-inch) pieces of green onion
1 (8-oz.) package frozen baby corn (24 ears)
1 cup hoisin sauce
1/2 cup plum sauce
1 teaspoon hot chili oil

1 teaspoon sesame oil
2 tablespoons soy sauce
2 tablespoons dry sherry wine
2 tablespoons honey
4 garlic cloves, finely chopped

Line a baking sheet with foil; set aside. Cut tenderloin in half crosswise, then into lengthwise 1/4-inch-thick slices. Pound slices gently between 2 pieces of waxed paper to 1/8 inch thickness. Cut each strip in half lengthwise again to approximately 5" x 1-1/2". Place a green-onion piece at narrow end of a meat strip; roll-up like a jelly roll. Alternate 3 meat rolls with 2 baby ears of corn on a 6-inch skewer. Arrange on foil-lined baking sheet. In a small bowl, combine hoisin sauce, plum sauce, chili oil, sesame oil, soy sauce, sherry wine, honey and garlic; blend well. Brush mixture over meat and corn; let stand 1 hour. Cook on a hot barbecue grill about 4 inches from heat 5 to 7 minutes or until brown on both sides. Baste once or twice during cooking. Serve warm with remaining sauce for dipping. Makes 12 servings.

Tip
Chili oil is an oil used in many hot, spicy Oriental dishes. The "heat" comes from the flavor of hot chilies. After opening the bottle, keep in a refrigerator for longer life.

Onion-Roquefort Roast Beef Pickups

*We used French rolls about six inches long. For smaller servings,
try the smaller pillow-shaped rolls.*

1 medium red onion, thinly sliced

4 ounces (about 1/2 cup) Roquefort or blue
cheese, crumbled

1/4 cup olive oil or vegetable oil

2 tablespoons red-wine vinegar

1 teaspoon chopped chives

1 tablespoon chopped fresh parsley

1 garlic clove, crushed

1 tablespoon steak sauce

1/4 teaspoon salt

1/8 teaspoon pepper

3 large (6-inch) French rolls, split

1/2 pound thinly sliced roast beef

Separate onion rings; place in a shallow non-metal container. Sprinkle with Roquefort or blue cheese. In a
small bowl, combine oil, vinegar, chives, parsley, garlic, steak sauce, salt and pepper. Pour mixture over
onions and cheese; toss to coat. Cover and refrigerate at least 2 hours. At serving time, drain onions and
cheese; save marinade. Arrange roast beef on each half of a French roll. Top with drained onions and
Roquefort cheese. Spoon additional marinade over top, if desired. Makes 6 open-faced servings.

Sweet & Spicy Smoked-Corned-Beef Cubes

*The smoky corned beef from the barbecue grill results in an
unusual taste. Ideal for dipping into spicy mustard sauce.*

1 garlic clove, crushed

1/2 teaspoon whole pickling spices

1 (1.12-oz.) can ground mustard

2 teaspoons cornstarch

1/8 teaspoon salt

1/3 cup cold water

1/3 cup white-wine vinegar

2/3 cup sugar

1 tablespoon peanut oil or vegetable oil

3-1/2 to 4 pounds corned-beef brisket

Cut a 4-inch square from 4 thicknesses of cheesecloth. Place garlic clove and pickling spices in center.
Gather corners and edges of cheesecloth; tie with string. In a 2-cup measure, thoroughly combine mustard,
cornstarch and salt; add water. Stir until dry ingredients are dissolved. In a small, heavy saucepan, combine
spice ball, vinegar, sugar and oil. Cook and stir over medium-low heat until sugar dissolves. Stir in mustard
mixture. Simmer over very low heat, stirring frequently, 15 to 20 minutes or until mixture thickens and
becomes a light-caramel color. Remove and discard spice ball; cover and refrigerate. Cook corned-beef
brisket according to package directions. About 15 minutes before brisket is done, light 6 or 7 charcoal
briquets. When hot, move coals to one side of barbecue unit; remove brisket from pan and place it on side of
grill that is opposite the hot briquets. Spread 6 to 8 hickory chips over hot coals; cover grill and smoke over low
heat about 45 minutes, adding wood chips to hot coals every 6 to 8 minutes. If necessary, add 3 or 4 charcoal
briquets after about 20 minutes of smoking. Remove brisket from grill; cut into 1-1/2-inch cubes. Serve on
small wooden picks; dip into sweet-mustard sauce. Makes 50 to 60 bite-sized servings.

Chicken-Stuffed Giant Shells

A great main dish at outdoor get-togethers.

10 to 12 giant pasta shells
1/4 cup dairy sour cream
1/4 cup mayonnaise
1 tablespoon finely chopped green onion
1 teaspoon prepared mustard
1 hard-cooked egg, chopped

2 tablespoons chopped sun-dried tomatoes in oil
1/4 teaspoon salt
1/8 teaspoon pepper
1 cup diced cooked chicken
1/2 cup (2 oz.) diced mozzarella cheese
2 tablespoons pine nuts or pistachios

In a 4-quart saucepan, bring 3 quarts salted water to a boil. Add pasta shells; cook 8 to 10 minutes or until barely tender. Immediately cover with cold water; drain well. In a medium bowl, combine sour cream, mayonnaise, green onion, mustard, egg, sun-dried tomatoes, salt and pepper. Stir in chicken and cheese. Spoon into cooked shells. Sprinkle pine nuts or pistachios on top. Serve immediately, or cover and refrigerate up to 24 hours. Makes 10 to 12 servings.

Grilled Chili-Dog Burritos

Everything is heated or cooked on the barbecue. Let the beans heat on the edge of the grill, while hot dogs cook over more intense coals.

1 (8-oz.) can refried beans
10 frankfurters
10 (5-inch) corn tortillas

3/4 cup (3 oz.) shredded Monterey Jack cheese
1 cup shredded lettuce

Heat beans in a small pan on a hot barbecue grill. Cut frankfurters lengthwise to within 1/4 inch of other side. Place on a hot grill 4 to 5 inches from heat. Cook 5 minutes or until hot and sizzling. At last minute, heat tortillas on grill. Turn when hot but still soft; heat other side. Place 1 frankfurter on each tortilla. Top with beans, cheese and lettuce; then with Fresh Salsa. Roll up tortilla. Makes 10 servings.

Fresh Salsa:

1 large tomato, chopped
1 California green chili or jalapeño pepper,
  chopped

1 teaspoon chopped cilantro
2 green onions, chopped
1/4 teaspoon salt

In a small bowl, combine tomato, green chili, cilantro, green onions and salt. Stir to blend. Refrigerate until ready to serve.

Stuffed Rice & Bean Salad

The total number of servings varies with the size of lettuce leaves. Allow about two tablespoons filling in small leaves; as much as 1/4 cup in large outside leaves.

1/2 cup dried pinto beans

3 cups water

1/2 cup (4 oz.) chopped ham

2 tablespoons chopped celery

1/4 cup chopped onion

1 teaspoon chili powder

1/4 teaspoon salt

2 or 3 dashes hot-pepper sauce

1/4 cup uncooked long-grain white rice

1 bunch leaf lettuce, such as butter or Bibb lettuce

In a large saucepan, combine pinto beans and water; bring to a boil 1 minute. Remove from heat; cover and let stand 1 hour. Add ham, celery, onion, chili powder, 1/4 teaspoon salt, hot-pepper sauce and uncooked rice. Cover and simmer 45 to 50 minutes or until beans and rice are tender; drain thoroughly. Pour Vinaigrette over cooked rice and beans; stir. Cover and refrigerate at least 2 hours or overnight. Drain rice mixture; spoon on individual lettuce leaves. Roll up. Garnish as desired. Serve immediately. Makes 10 to 15 servings.

Vinaigrette:

1/3 cup vegetable oil

2 tablespoons red-wine vinegar

1-1/2 teaspoons Dijon-style mustard

1/4 teaspoon salt

1/8 teaspoon pepper

1 tablespoon finely chopped cilantro

In a small bowl, combine all ingredients until well blended.

Green 'n' Gold Walk-Away Salad

Either leaf lettuce or the salad-bowl variety is pliable enough to wrap around these salad ingredients. Large outside leaves should be halved before filling. (Photo on cover.)

4 medium zucchini, shredded

1/2 teaspoon salt

1/2 cup dairy sour cream

2 tablespoons chopped green onion

1 tablespoon chopped fresh parsley

1/2 teaspoon dried leaf tarragon, crushed

1/8 teaspoon pepper

2 teaspoons red-wine vinegar

1 medium carrot, peeled, shredded

10 to 12 medium lettuce leaves

In a strainer, combine zucchini and salt; let stand 5 minutes. Press out liquid with the back of a spoon. In a large bowl, combine sour cream, green onion, parsley, tarragon, pepper and vinegar. Add drained zucchini and carrot; toss until well blended. Spoon 2 to 3 tablespoons salad in center of each lettuce leaf; roll up. Serve immediately. Makes 10 to 12 servings.

Shangri-La Drumsticks, page 123, and Stuffed Rice & Bean Salad, above.

◆

Mustardy Asparagus Wrap-Arounds

Take advantage of this treat when slender fresh asparagus is available in the grocery store or at a produce stand.

18 small fresh asparagus spears (about 1/2 lb.)
1-1/2 cups chicken stock or bouillon

6 slices ham or mortadella (about 5 to 6 ounces)
1 tablespoon sweet-hot mustard

Trim asparagus. Cook asparagus in stock 4 to 6 minutes or until barely tender; drain well. Spread mustard on 1 side of a ham slice. Top with 3 spears cooked asparagus; roll up. Repeat with remaining ingredients. Serve immediately. Makes 6 servings.

Deli-Potato-Salad Wrap-Ups

Stop by your favorite delicatessen and choose several special kinds of cold cuts.

3 medium potatoes, cooked, peeled, cut in
   julienne strips
1 cup (4 oz.) diced Cheddar cheese
1/2 cup diced celery
1/2 cup mayonnaise
1 tablespoon prepared mustard
1 teaspoon prepared horseradish

1 tablespoon vinegar
1 teaspoon sugar
1 teaspoon salt
1/4 teaspoon pepper
15 to 20 large thin slices salami or other cold
   sliced meat

In a large bowl, combine potato strips, cheese and celery. In a small bowl, combine mayonnaise, mustard, horseradish, vinegar, sugar, salt and pepper. Spoon mayonnaise mixture over potato mixture, tossing to blend. Cover and refrigerate at least 2 hours. Spoon 2 to 3 tablespoons potato salad along center of each slice of cold meat; roll up. Serve immediately. Makes 15 to 20 servings.

Vegetable-Cheese Pita Pickups

A salad in a pocket that you can pick up.

3 (8-inch) pita bread rounds, cut in half
1 (8-oz.) package soft cream cheese
1 small cucumber, cut in 36 thin slices
Freshly ground black pepper

1 medium green bell pepper, cut in 36 slivers
6 large leaves romaine lettuce
1/4 cup thinly sliced green onions
6 tablespoons (1.5 oz.) crumbled blue cheese

Carefully open pita bread halves; spread about 2 tablespoons cream cheese inside each pita half. In each half, place 6 cucumber slices. Sprinkle generously with black pepper. Top with 6 slivers of green pepper and a piece of lettuce leaf. Sprinkle green onions and blue cheese over top. Makes 6 servings.

Pesto-Stuffed Cherry Tomatoes

A colorful and appetizing addition to a tray of fresh vegetables, or an interesting contrast of flavors when served with grilled chicken.
(Photo on cover.)

1/2 cup lightly packed fresh basil leaves
1/4 cup lightly packed fresh parsley leaves
1/4 cup (3/4 oz.) grated Parmesan cheese
1/4 teaspoon salt
1/8 teaspoon pepper

2 tablespoons olive oil
1 garlic clove, coarsely chopped
1/2 cup (4 oz.) ricotta cheese
20 cherry tomatoes

In a blender or food processor fitted with the metal blade, combine basil, parsley, Parmesan cheese, salt, pepper, olive oil and garlic. Process until finely chopped. Stir in ricotta cheese. Make an "X" cut in bottom of each tomato almost to stem end. Gently open tomato, being careful not to tear. Spoon or pipe about 2 teaspoons mixture into each tomato. Makes 20 stuffed tomatoes.

Chicken Barrel Roll-Ups

*A package of thin uncooked turkey cutlets makes a good
substitute for chicken.*

1 to 1-1/4 pounds boneless chicken breasts,
  skinned
1 cup ground cooked ham
2 cups soft bread crumbs

1 cup (4 oz.) shredded Cheddar cheese
1 tablespoon finely chopped green onion
1 teaspoon prepared mustard
1 egg, beaten slightly

Partially freeze chicken to make it easier to slice. Lightly pound chicken with a meat mallet for an even thickness. With a sharp knife, make 28 to 30 thin lengthwise slices; set aside. In a medium bowl, combine ham, bread crumbs, cheese, green onion, mustard and egg. Form 1 tablespoon bread mixture into a barrel shape about 1-1/4 inches long. Wrap in a strip of chicken breast. Repeat until all mixture is used. Thread 3 or 4 rolls on a 10- to 12-inch metal skewer. Place on a barbecue grill or under oven broiler 4 to 5 inches from heat source. Brush with Tarragon-Butter Sauce. Cook 5 minutes. Brush with sauce; turn kabobs. Cook another 4 to 5 minutes or until done. Makes 28 to 30 roll-ups.

Tarragon-Butter Sauce:

1/3 cup butter or margarine, melted
1 tablespoon white-wine vinegar
1 tablespoon lemon juice

1 tablespoon finely chopped fresh tarragon
1/4 teaspoon salt
1/8 teaspoon pepper

In a small bowl, combine all ingredients; stir to blend well.

Parma Eggs

*Similar to deviled eggs with the addition of spicy ingredients for an
Italian influence.*

6 hard-cooked eggs
1 tablespoon finely chopped sun-dried tomatoes in
  oil
1-1/2 teaspoons sweet-hot mustard

1/3 cup finely chopped prosciutto
1/4 cup mayonnaise
Italian parsley for garnish

Cut hard-cooked eggs in half lengthwise; remove yolks. Set egg-white halves aside. In a medium bowl, mash yolks with a fork. Stir in tomatoes, mustard, prosciutto and mayonnaise. Spoon egg-yolk mixture into reserved egg-white halves. Garnish with sprigs of Italian parsley. Makes 12 egg halves.

Picnic Pointers

Picnicking is a delightful form of recreation enjoyed by people worldwide. Americans somehow seem to find more reasons and places to practice this art. They picnic in the mountains, at the seashore, in parks, in motor homes, on sand dunes, at sporting events, at open-air concerts—in fact, any place where a tablecloth can be spread. Even the tablecloth is not a necessity.

A few minutes of planning is perhaps the best assurance of an enjoyable picnic, devoid of disappointments, frustrations and that familiar quote, "I wish I had . . . ." From a convenience and sanitation standpoint, it is far better to prepare as much of your picnic food as possible in your own kitchen. Conveniences are usually scarce at picnic sites.

Decide what foods will be served at each course. Unless you're sure of maintaining cold foods at about 40F (5C) or below, it is best to avoid foods high in protein and moisture. These include milk, cream, poultry, fish, shellfish, eggs, mayonnaise, cream pies and other such foods. These foods are especially susceptible to bacterial growth and can cause illness if not kept cool.

Select and wash containers in which foods or drink will be transported. Plan ways to keep hot items hot and cold items cold. Thermal bottles or jugs in 1-pint to 2-gallon capacity can be used to transport cold food or drink. These bottles should be chilled with ice water for at least 5 minutes. Pour out water and fill immediately with chilled food or drink. Close tops securely.

An ice chest or cooler is most practical for transporting cold foods and bottled or canned drinks. All cold foods and drinks should be chilled in their containers in your refrigerator before being placed in an ice chest. Close lid securely. Refrigerants for ice chests include:

Ice Over Food Containers: Place chilled food containers with lids in chest. Pour ice cubes or crushed ice over containers. This is perhaps the most efficient method to ensure uniform cooling. But a word of caution—food containers must be tightly sealed to avoid water seeping in.

Ice & Salt Mixture: An empty 3-pound coffee or shortening can filled with ice and salt makes an excellent refrigerant. Place a layer of ice cubes or a 1-inch layer of crushed ice in can. Sprinkle ice with two tablespoons salt. Continue layering alternately with ice and salt until full. Place lid securely on can. Place filled can upright on a piece of foil in center of ice chest and arrange cooled food containers around and on top of can.

Frozen Water-Filled Containers & Ice Substitutes: Water-filled containers can be empty milk cartons or similar containers that have been washed and filled with water to 1-1/2 inches from top. Seal with tape and freeze. Commercial ice-substitutes or nontoxic gels can be purchased at most supermarkets and frozen. Place these containers in your ice chest and arrange chilled food containers among ice containers.

Dry Ice: Dry ice or carbon dioxide is best used for keeping ice cream and other frozen desserts below 32F (0C). Dry ice can be purchased at some ice-cream and liquor stores and at most ice plants. It should be handled with gloves to avoid burns and should be wrapped in heavy paper. For best results, tape wrapped dry ice to inside lid of ice chest or place on top of frozen food. Do not inhale fumes.

To carry hot food to a picnic site, try to time the cooking so that food is done just prior to departure. Foods can be transported hot for several hours in the containers in which they were cooked. The container should have a tight-fitting lid and must be well insulated immediately after it is removed from the stove or oven. Using pot holders or gloves, wrap hot container first in two thicknesses of foil and then in at least five layers of newspapers. Secure wrapping with tape. Longer preservation can be achieved by placing the wrapped food container in an empty ice chest.

Hot food can be transported to the picnic in a thermal bottle or jug. Bottle or jug should be preheated with boiling water at least 5 minutes. Pour out hot water and fill with hot food; close top.

Finally, select and pack condiments, garnishes, equipment and supplies. Except for perishables, most items can be packed in a picnic basket or sturdy box.

Special Celebrations

Holidays and special events provide us with an excuse to prepare foods that are designed to fit the spirit of the occasion. It may be Herbed Party Sandwiches or Savory Goat-Cheese Bars for a wedding reception or anniversary party.

For Yuletide parties, we enjoy New Zealand Fruitcake Squares. We discovered this kind of fruitcake when we visited Auckland. After borrowing the traditional recipe from our friend, we adapted it to a square baking pan; then cut it into small squares and served it in festive bon-bon cups.

Lattice Almond-Berry Heart is a sure way to impress family or guests on Valentine's Day. The base is made of heart-shaped sugar-cookie dough that's spread with strawberry jam; then topped with a cookie lattice.

For Halloween, there's a choice of crunchy Chocolate-Meringue Pumpkin Faces or quick and easy Nacho Cheese Pita Jack-O'-Lanterns. The Meringues are baked so require several hours for mixing and cooking. If you're short of time, take advantage of the pita recipe. Use your ingenuity to cut out weird faces in pita rounds; then season with the spicy prepared dip mix, and bake for a few minutes. Substitute other dry packaged dip mixes if the nacho flavor is too hot for you.

Lattice Almond-Berry Heart

It's so impressive for such a minimum of effort! Use it as a Valentine centerpiece or at a bridal shower or wedding-anniversary celebration. (Photo on previous pages.)

1/3 cup butter or margarine, room temperature

2/3 cup sugar

1 egg, separated

3 tablespoons milk

1/2 teaspoon vanilla extract

1-3/4 cups all-purpose flour

1/2 teaspoon baking powder

1/8 teaspoon salt

2/3 cup strawberry jam or raspberry jam

1 teaspoon water

1 teaspoon sugar

2 tablespoons finely chopped almonds

Preheat oven to 350F (175C). Line a 9-inch heart-shaped pan with foil; grease foil. In a large bowl, cream butter and 2/3 cup sugar; beat in egg yolk, milk and vanilla. Stir in flour, baking powder and salt. Divide dough in half. Press half the dough evenly on bottom of prepared pan. Spread with jam. Roll remaining dough to a 10-inch circle. Cut into a heart shape using pan as a pattern. Cut 1-inch-wide diagonal strips across the heart. Place the strips 1-inch apart on the jam to resemble a lattice. In a small cup, combine egg white and water; brush lattice with egg-white mixture. Sprinkle with 1 teaspoon sugar and almonds. Bake in preheated oven 30 minutes or until lightly browned. Cool 10 minutes in pan. Remove cookie; cool on a rack about 1 hour. Carefully remove foil. Cool completely. Cut into individual pieces. Makes 1 (9-inch) heart.

Red-Hot Popcorn Heart

What a beautiful, edible centerpiece for Valentine celebrations. The only problem is that you may hesitate to eat it because it's so interesting.

8 cups popped popcorn

1 cup sugar

1/3 cup light corn syrup

1/3 cup water

1/4 cup butter or margarine

1/3 cup red cinnamon candies

Place popcorn in a large heat-proof bowl. Butter a 9-inch heart-shaped pan. In a medium saucepan, combine sugar, corn syrup, water and butter. Cook over medium heat, stirring, until mixture reaches 250F (121C) or the hard-ball stage when dropped into cold water. Remove from heat; quickly stir in cinnamon candies. Immediately pour mixture over popcorn, tossing until well coated. Using a spatula or the back of a spoon, press mixture firmly into prepared pan. Cool on a rack. Run spatula around edge to loosen; remove from pan. Pull apart to eat. Makes 1 (9-inch) heart.

Snowcap Raspberry Finger-Puffs

*So eye-appealing that you'll make them for bridal showers or
Valentine parties. For a more festive look, top the glaze with
pastel sprinkles or pink crystal sugar.*

1/4 cup butter or margarine	1/8 teaspoon salt
1/2 cup water	2 eggs
1/2 cup all-purpose flour	

Preheat oven to 400F (205C). Lightly grease a baking sheet. In a medium saucepan, heat butter and water to a rolling boil. Add flour and salt all at once; stir vigorously over low heat 1 minute or until mixture becomes smooth and does not cling to side of pan. Remove from heat; beat in eggs, 1 at a time. Fit a pastry bag with a plain round 1/2-inch tip; fill bag with flour mixture. Pipe mixture onto prepared baking sheet into finger-like strips about 2-1/2" x 1". Bake in preheated oven 15 to 20 minutes or until golden. Cool; split each eclair. Fill with Raspberry Filling. Replace lids. Spoon Snowcap Glaze over top. Refrigerate until serving time. Makes 16 servings.

Raspberry Filling:

1 cup fresh or frozen unsweetened raspberries	1 teaspoon unflavored gelatin powder
1/2 cup sugar	1/2 cup whipping cream

In a blender or food processor fitted with the metal blade, puree raspberries; strain to remove seeds. In a small saucepan, combine sugar and gelatin; stir in strained raspberries. Cook over medium heat, stirring until sugar dissolves; cool to lukewarm. In a medium bowl, whip cream until stiff peaks form. Fold in raspberry mixture.

Snowcap Glaze:

3 ounces white chocolate, chopped	3 tablespoons sugar
1 tablespoon milk	

In a small saucepan over low heat, melt white chocolate. In another small saucepan, heat milk almost to boiling; add sugar, stirring until dissolved. Pour milk mixture into melted white chocolate; stir until smooth.

Hazelnut Tarts with Raspberry Glaze

They're small but rich; just right for a grand finale dessert after an important dinner.

1/2 cup butter, chilled	1/4 teaspoon salt
1-1/2 cups all-purpose flour	3 to 4 tablespoons cold water

Cut chilled butter into 1/2-inch slices. In a medium bowl, combine flour and salt. Add butter; with a pastry blender or fork, cut in butter until mixture resembles coarse crumbs. Sprinkle water over dough; stir with a fork to blend. Form into a flattened ball. Wrap pastry; refrigerate 1 hour. On a lightly floured board, roll out pastry to 1/8 inch thick. Cut pastry into 20 to 25 circles or ovals. Carefully fit each into a miniature oval or round tart pan. Trim edges; prick pastry sides and bottom with a fork. Freeze while preparing filling. To fill, place pastry-lined pans on a shallow baking pan; bake in preheated oven 10 to 12 minutes or until firm but not brown. Spoon about 1 tablespoon hazelnut filling into each pastry shell. Return to oven. Bake 8 minutes or until golden. Cool 5 minutes. Spoon a thin layer of raspberry glaze over warm tarts. Makes 20 to 25 tarts.

Hazelnut Filling:

1/2 cup hazelnuts	1/3 cup butter, room temperature
1/4 cup sugar	2 eggs

Preheat oven to 400F (205C). Place hazelnuts in a shallow baking pan. Bake in preheated oven 6 minutes or until skins begin to crack. Wrap nuts in a clean towel; let stand 2 minutes. Rub nuts briskly with towel to remove most of the dark skins. In a blender or food processor fitted with the metal blade, combine hazelnuts and sugar. Process until nuts are finely chopped. In a medium bowl, beat butter until fluffy; beat in hazelnut mixture and eggs.

Raspberry Glaze:

1/4 cup raspberry preserves
1 tablespoon raspberry liqueur

In a small bowl, combine raspberry preserves and liqueur. Strain, discarding seeds.

Tropical Stacks

After stacks are firm, place each in a bon-bon paper. A perfect confection for a gift or special party.

1 (12-oz.) package white-chocolate pieces (about 2 cups)

2 tablespoons orange juice

1/2 teaspoon grated orange peel

1 tablespoon finely chopped crystallized ginger

3/4 cup finely chopped dates

1/2 cup flaked coconut

Line 2 baking sheets or trays with waxed paper. In a medium saucepan, combine white-chocolate pieces and orange juice. Heat over low heat, stirring until chocolate melts. Remove from heat; add orange peel, ginger, dates and coconut. Refrigerate 5 minutes, if necessary to hold shape. Drop by heaping teaspoons on waxed paper. Refrigerate until firm. Makes 30 to 33 pieces.

Chocolate-Mint Sandwiches

The perfect answer to super-quick cookies with a festive look. With green-sugar topping, they'll fit into St. Patrick's Day celebrations as well as Christmas.

1 (20-oz.) package refrigerator sugar-cookie dough

18 cream-filled chocolate-mint patties

Green sugar

Freeze cookie dough about 1 hour. Preheat oven to 375F (190C). Cut dough into 1/4-inch-thick crosswise slices. Place a mint patty on half the slices. Top with remaining cookie slices. Press edges to seal. Place cookies, 2 inches apart, on an ungreased baking sheet. Sprinkle with green sugar. Bake in preheated oven 10 to 12 minutes or until lightly browned. Makes 18 cookies.

Seashell Madeleine Cookies

*Tiny shell-shaped cookie sandwiches with filling oozing out look
like miniature sea creatures. A surprisingly impressive presentation
for a fancy tea or reception.*

2 eggs

1/3 cup sugar

1/4 cup butter or margarine, melted, cooled

1/2 teaspoon grated lemon peel

1/2 cup all-purpose flour

Preheat oven to 400F (205C). Grease a 1-1/2 inch shell-shaped madeleine pan. In a medium bowl, beat eggs about 3 minutes or until thickened. Gradually add sugar, beating until light colored and thick. Fold in slightly cooled butter and lemon peel. Fold in flour. Fill each shell about 3/4 full. Bake in preheated oven 10 minutes or until golden. Carefully remove from pan; cool on a rack. Repeat with remaining dough. When cookies are cool, spread filling on the smooth side of half the cookies. Top each filled cookie with an unfilled cookie, smooth-side down, making a cookie sandwich. Makes about 26 small seashell-cookie sandwiches.

Seashell Filling:

1 cup powdered sugar

2 tablespoons unsweetened cocoa powder

2 tablespoons butter or margarine, melted

1/4 teaspoon vanilla extract

1 tablespoon milk

Sift powdered sugar and cocoa powder into a small bowl. Add melted butter, vanilla and milk; beat until smooth.

Spicy Holiday Thumbprints

A festive version of the ever-popular thumbprint cookie. Sift powdered sugar over top for a more "snowy" look.

3/4 cup lightly packed brown sugar
3/4 cup butter or margarine, room temperature
2 cups all-purpose flour
1/2 teaspoon ground allspice

1/4 teaspoon ground ginger
1/2 teaspoon ground cinnamon
1/4 teaspoon salt
2 tablespoons milk

Preheat oven to 350F (175C). In a large bowl, cream brown sugar and butter until fluffy. Beat in flour, allspice, ginger, cinnamon, salt and milk. Shape mixture into 1-inch balls. Place balls about 2 inches apart on ungreased baking sheets. With your thumb, make an indentation in center of each. Bake in preheated oven 10 to 12 minutes or until almost firm but not brown. Spoon about 3/4 teaspoon Holiday Cheese Filling in center of each cookie. Return to oven; bake 3 to 4 minutes or until edges begin to brown. Makes 60 to 65 cookies.

Holiday Cheese Filling:

1 (3-oz.) package cream cheese, room temperature
1 cup sifted powdered sugar

2 tablespoons all-purpose flour
1/4 cup chopped walnuts
1/2 cup chopped candied fruit

In a small bowl, combine cream cheese, powdered sugar and flour until smooth. Stir in nuts and candied fruit.

Orange-Mincemeat Loaf

The texture of this loaf is similar to a nut bread; orange juice and mincemeat add new interest for holiday entertaining.

2 eggs
1/2 cup lightly packed brown sugar
1/3 cup milk
1/3 cup orange juice
1/4 cup butter or margarine, melted

1 cup prepared mincemeat
1 teaspoon baking powder
1/2 teaspoon baking soda
2-1/4 cups all-purpose flour

Preheat oven to 350F (175C). Grease a 9" x 5" loaf pan. In a large bowl, beat eggs and brown sugar until well blended. Beat in milk, orange juice and melted butter; add mincemeat. Stir in baking powder, baking soda and flour. Spoon into prepared pan. Bake in preheated oven 1 hour or until a wooden pick inserted in center comes out clean. Cool in pan 10 minutes; invert on a cooling rack. Cool completely; slice. Makes 1 loaf.

Glazed Holiday Fruit Bars

*It's worth the extra effort to caramelize the sugar to dress up fruits
and nuts with a special look and taste for the holiday season.*

1/2 cup butter or margarine, room temperature
3/4 cup sugar
1 egg
1/4 teaspoon almond extract
1/4 cup half and half

1/4 teaspoon grated lemon peel
1 teaspoon baking powder
1-1/2 cups all-purpose flour
Red and green candied cherry halves for garnish

Grease a 13" x 9" baking pan. In a large bowl, beat butter and 3/4 cup sugar until light and fluffy. Beat in egg, almond extract and half and half. Stir in lemon peel, baking powder and flour. Spread into bottom of prepared pan. Refrigerate while preparing topping. Preheat oven to 375F (190C). Spread topping over cookie dough in pan. Bake in preheated oven 20 minutes or until golden brown. Remove from oven; cool on a rack. Cut into 1-1/2- to 2-inch bars. Top each bar with half a red or green candied cherry. Makes 25 to 30 bars.

Topping:

1 cup sugar
1/4 cup butter or margarine
2/3 cup half and half, warmed

1 cup chopped candied fruit
1/2 cup coarsely chopped cashews or pecans

In a 9-inch heavy skillet, melt sugar over medium heat until it is a light-caramel-colored liquid. Remove from heat; slowly and carefully stir in butter and half and half. Return to low heat to completely dissolve sugar. Add candied fruit and nuts.

Cranberry-White-Chocolate Cereal Bars

*These bars can be used as an easy-to-make gift from your kitchen
or confection to serve as a special treat for holiday entertaining.*

12 ounces white chocolate
1/2 cup canned whole-berry cranberry sauce
3 cups doughnut-shaped oat cereal
1/4 cup chopped peanuts

2 teaspoons vegetable oil
1/2 cup sifted powdered sugar
2 tablespoons milk

Line bottom and sides of a 9" x 5" loaf pan with foil. In a medium saucepan, melt 6 ounces chocolate and cranberry sauce over medium heat. Stir in cereal and peanuts. Press half of mixture into prepared loaf pan. Reserve remaining half for top layer. In a small saucepan, combine remaining 6 ounces white chocolate, oil, powdered sugar and milk. Heat, stirring over low heat, until smooth. Spread over bottom layer of cereal in pan. Top with remaining cereal mixture. Chill until firm. Remove from pan. Cut into slices. Makes 1 loaf or about 24 slices.

New Zealand Fruitcake Squares

When we visited our friend, Tui Flower in New Zealand, she introduced us to fruitcake with more emphasis on raisins and currants than candied fruit. We were so impressed that we borrowed her recipe and adapted it for this book.

1 cup seedless raisins
1 cup golden raisins
1 cup currants
1/3 cup candied cherries, quartered
1/4 cup chopped candied orange peel
1 cup all-purpose flour
1/8 teaspoon baking soda
1/8 teaspoon ground allspice
1/8 teaspoon ground cinnamon
1/8 teaspoon ground nutmeg

1/8 teaspoon ground ginger
1/2 cup butter, room temperature
1/2 cup lightly packed brown sugar
2 eggs
1 tablespoon molasses
1 teaspoon grated lemon peel
1/4 teaspoon vanilla extract
1/4 cup brandy
Sliced candied cherries for garnish

Preheat oven to 275F (135C). Line bottom and sides of an 8-inch-square baking pan with 2 layers of brown paper. Grease layer next to cake. In a large bowl, combine raisins, currants, cherries and orange peel. Add flour, baking soda and spices; toss to coat fruits. In a large bowl, cream butter and brown sugar. Beat in eggs, 1 at a time. Stir in molasses, lemon peel and vanilla. Stir in flour-coated fruits. Spoon into prepared pan; smooth top with back of a spoon. Bake in preheated oven 1 to 1-1/4 hours or until center springs back when gently pressed with your finger tip. Cool to room temperature. Pierce with a skewer at 1/2-inch intervals over top. Drizzle about 2 tablespoons brandy over top. Remove cake from pan. Moisten a piece of cheesecloth with remaining brandy; wrap around cake, then wrap cake in foil. Refrigerate wrapped cake at least 2 weeks before using. Cut into 1- to 1-1/4-inch squares. Place each in a bon-bon paper. Garnish with sliced candied cherries. Makes 40 to 50 squares.

Double Chocolate-Pecan Treats

*Rich and moist; almost like a brownie. Make them in individual
quiche pans or assorted shapes of miniature baking pans
generally used for small fruit tarts. A welcome addition to a
graduation party or open-house.*

3 ounces semisweet chocolate

1/2 cup butter or margarine

3 eggs

1 cup sugar

1/2 cup all-purpose flour

1/4 teaspoon salt

1/2 cup chopped pecans

Pecan halves for garnish

Preheat oven to 350F (175C). In a small saucepan, melt chocolate and butter over low heat. In a medium bowl, beat eggs with sugar. Beat in flour and salt, then melted chocolate mixture. Stir in chopped pecans. Pour into 2-1/2-inch tart pans or 3-1/2-inch quiche pans. Bake in preheated oven 15 to 20 minutes or until firm in center. Cool; gently loosen sides with knife. Turn upside down. Spread bottom of each cake with Creamy Chocolate Topping. Garnish with pecan halves. Makes 24 to 30 (2-1/2-inch) or 16 to 18 (3-1/2-inch) servings.

Creamy Chocolate Topping:

2 tablespoons butter or margarine, melted

2 tablespoons unsweetened cocoa powder

1/4 teaspoon vanilla extract

1-1/2 tablespoons milk

1 cup sifted powdered sugar

In a small bowl, stir together topping ingredients until smooth and creamy.

Nacho Cheese Pita Jack-O'-Lanterns

Spicy Halloween treats that are easy to make. Use the dry dip mix right from the package without reconstituting it or adding other ingredients.

4 (6-inch) pita bread rounds
2 tablespoons vegetable oil

1 (1-1/8-oz.) package nacho cheese sauce and dip mix

Preheat oven to 350F (175C). Lightly grease 2 baking sheets. Horizontally split each pita bread into 2 rounds. Cut out a face on each. Brush entire surface lightly with oil. Place on waxed paper; sift dry cheese mix over each. Transfer to prepared baking sheets. Bake 10 to 12 minutes or until edges begin to brown. Serve warm or at room temperature. Makes 8 Jack-O'-Lanterns.

Chocolate-Meringue Pumpkin Faces

Here's your opportunity to make many unusual kinds of faces with different shaped eyes, noses and mouths.

3 egg whites, room temperature
1/4 teaspoon cream of tartar
1/2 teaspoon vanilla extract
3/4 cup granulated sugar
15 drops orange food coloring
1/2 cup sifted powdered sugar

1 tablespoon unsweetened cocoa powder
2 teaspoons butter or margarine, room temperature
1/4 teaspoon vanilla extract
2 teaspoons milk

Preheat oven to 275F (135C). Line 2 large baking sheets with parchment paper or brown paper. Draw 5 (3-inch) circles on each. Using an electric mixer and a medium bowl, beat egg whites, cream of tartar and 1/2 teaspoon vanilla until foamy. Gradually beat in granulated sugar, beating until very stiff and glossy. Fold in food coloring. Spread meringue in circles on baking sheets; smooth tops flat. Form a stem at one end of each. Bake in preheated oven 1 hour. Turn oven off; leave in oven with door closed 1 additional hour. Cool; remove from paper. In a small bowl, combine powdered sugar, cocoa powder, butter, 1/4 teaspoon vanilla and milk. Add a few drops of milk, if necessary, to make the right spreading consistency. Using a narrow spatula or a pastry tube, decorate meringues by making eyes, nose and mouth. If desired, cover stem with frosting. Makes 10 faces.

Herbed Party Sandwiches

Get out your fancy cutters for party shapes. Arrange finished
open-faced sandwiches on your prettiest serving tray.

1-1/2 tablespoons chopped fresh tarragon
1-1/2 tablespoons chopped chives
1/4 cup chopped watercress
1-1/2 tablespoons chopped fresh dill
1 cup mayonnaise
30 to 40 thin slices pumpernickel bread

15 to 20 small cooked, shelled shrimp
Fresh dill sprigs for garnish
15 to 20 small slices cooked chicken
Fresh tarragon sprigs for garnish
Red-pepper strips for garnish, optional

In a food processor fitted with the metal blade, combine tarragon, chives, watercress and dill; add mayonnaise. Process until herbs are finely chopped and blended with mayonnaise. Cut bread into small hearts, diamonds, rounds or a shape that fits the occasion. Spread each bread shape with 1/2 to 1 teaspoon herbed mayonnaise. Halve shrimp lengthwise, starting along back. Arrange two halves, cut-side down, on 15 to 20 open-faced sandwiches. Garnish with fresh dill. Arrange 1 slice cooked chicken and a small sprig of fresh tarragon on each of remaining sandwiches. Garnish with red-pepper strips, if desired. Makes 30 to 40 open-faced sandwiches.

Caviar-Topped Filo Cups

Remove hot filo cups to cooling rack about 5 minutes after they
come out of oven. This keeps filo cups at their crispy best.

1/2 cup (4 oz.) small-curd cottage cheese
1 egg
2 tablespoons all-purpose flour
1/4 teaspoon baking powder
1 teaspoon lemon juice
1/2 teaspoon Worcestershire sauce
1 teaspoon chopped chives
1/4 teaspoon salt

1/8 teaspoon pepper
1/2 cup dairy sour cream
1/4 cup butter or margarine, melted
3 sheets filo dough
2 hard-cooked eggs, chopped
2 tablespoons dairy sour cream
1 to 2 tablespoons golden or black caviar
Small strips of chives

Preheat oven to 375F (190C). In a medium bowl, beat cottage cheese until almost smooth. Beat in egg, flour, baking powder, lemon juice, Worcestershire sauce, chives, salt and pepper. Stir in sour cream; set aside. Brush melted butter over 1 side of each sheet of filo. Fold in half; brush again and fold again to form quarter-sheets. Cut each quarter-sheet into 6 equal pieces. Gently press into miniature muffin cups. Fill with about 2 teaspoons cheese mixture. Bake in preheated oven 15 minutes or until filo is golden and filling is set. Top each cup with a little hard-cooked egg, about 1/3 teaspoon sour cream, a dab of caviar and several strips of chives. Serve warm. Makes 18 servings.

Layered Pesto Spread

*Impressive two-layer spread, consisting of green base and
off-white top. For a festive look at holiday time, we sprinkle the top
with additional chopped parsley and chives; then add red accents
to the tray with clusters of cherry tomatoes.*

4 ounces Roquefort or blue cheese, crumbled
1/2 cup (4 oz.) ricotta cheese
2 tablespoons butter or margarine, melted
1/2 cup coarsely chopped fresh basil
1 garlic clove, chopped
1 (8-oz.) package cream cheese, room
   temperature

3 tablespoons coarsely chopped fresh parsley
2 tablespoons grated Parmesan cheese
1/3 cup pine nuts
2 tablespoons chopped chives
Crackers or French bread

Line a 3- or 4-cup mold with plastic wrap. In a small bowl, combine Roquefort cheese, ricotta cheese and butter. Spoon into lined mold; press lightly with the back of a spoon. In a blender or food processor fitted with the metal blade, combine basil, garlic, cream cheese, parsley, Parmesan cheese, pine nuts and chives. Process until well mixed but not smooth. Spoon over Roquefort mixture; press lightly. Cover and refrigerate at least 2 hours. To unmold, invert onto a serving tray; remove plastic wrap. Spread mixture on crackers or French bread. Makes about 3 cups spread.

Open-Faced Salmon-Caper Sandwiches

*Designed to impress guests at special parties. For a bridal shower
or wedding reception, cut bread in shape of hearts, bells or other
designs to fit the occasion.*

1/3 cup dairy sour cream
1 (3-oz.) package cream cheese, room
   temperature
1 (3-oz.) package smoked salmon (lox), cut in
   small pieces
1 tablespoon chopped fresh dill
1 teaspoon lemon juice

1 teaspoon chopped chives
2 tablespoons capers, drained, chopped
30 to 40 thin slices party rye or pumpernickel
   bread
Fresh dill for garnish
Whole capers for garnish

In a food processor fitted with the metal blade, combine sour cream, cream cheese, salmon, dill, lemon juice and chives. Process until well blended. Stir in capers. Cut bread into desired shapes. Spread mixture on bread. Garnish with dill and additional whole capers. Makes 30 to 40 servings.

Cold Meat Party Carousel

*Get out your prettiest tray for this party platter. It's an impressive
idea for holiday parties or family reunions. Long, thin, Italian-style
bread sticks are especially appealing; thin slices of roast beef
make an interesting change.*

2 tablespoons Dijon-style mustard
1/3 cup dairy sour cream
1/3 cup mayonnaise
1 garlic clove, minced
1/4 teaspoon salt
1 teaspoon green peppercorns, drained, slightly
   crushed

8 to 10 slices salami
8 to 10 slices mortadella
8 to 10 slices cooked pastrami
24 to 30 bread sticks
Tomato rose for garnish

In a small bowl, combine mustard, sour cream, mayonnaise, garlic and salt. Stir in peppercorns. Cover and refrigerate at least 1 hour. Spread about 1 to 1-1/2 teaspoons mustard mixture on each slice of salami, mortadella and pastrami. Roll each around one bread stick. Arrange, seam-side down, in a spoke design on a round tray. Garnish with a tomato rose. Makes 24 to 30 servings.

Crab-Stuffed Artichoke Bottoms

*A sumptuous dish for special celebrations! Be sure to use
water-packed artichoke bottoms. The marinated ones are too spicy
and tart for this recipe.*

1-1/2 tablespoons butter or margarine
1 tablespoon all-purpose flour
1/4 teaspoon dry mustard
1/4 teaspoon salt
1/8 teaspoon white pepper
Pinch ground red pepper
3 tablespoons chopped green onions
1/4 cup half and half
1/8 teaspoon Worcestershire sauce

1 tablespoon sherry
1 egg white, beaten until frothy
2 teaspoons finely chopped green bell pepper
6 ounces crabmeat, cut into small pieces
2 (14-oz.) cans artichoke bottoms or crowns,
   well-drained
1 tablespoon butter or margarine, melted
Paprika

Preheat oven to 450F (230C). In a medium saucepan, melt 1-1/2 tablespoons butter; stir in flour, dry mustard, salt, white pepper and red pepper. Add green onions. Gradually stir in half and half; bring to a boil, stirring constantly. Remove from heat. Stir in Worcestershire sauce, sherry and egg white. Fold in green bell pepper and crabmeat. Brush artichoke bottoms with 1 tablespoon melted butter. Spoon about 1 tablespoon crabmeat mixture into artichoke bottoms. Sprinkle lightly with paprika. Place on a baking sheet; bake, uncovered, in preheated oven 10 minutes or until hot. Makes 12 to 16 servings.

Savory Goat-Cheese Bars

Perfect for a crowd. Choose two or more toppings and arrange in alternate rows.

1-1/3 cups all-purpose flour
1/2 teaspoon salt
1/4 cup toasted sesame seeds
1/2 cup vegetable shortening
3 tablespoons cold water
1 (8-oz.) package cream cheese, room
   temperature
3 eggs

7 to 8 ounces goat cheese, diced
2 tablespoons finely chopped sun-dried tomatoes
   in oil
1/4 teaspoon dried leaf marjoram, crushed
1/4 teaspoon fines herbes
1/2 teaspoon salt
1/2 cup half and half

Preheat oven to 425F (220C). Line sides and bottom of a 13" x 9" baking pan with foil. In a medium bowl, combine flour, salt and sesame seeds. With a pastry blender or fork, cut in shortening until mixture resembles coarse crumbs. Add water, 1 tablespoon at a time, while blending mixture with a fork. Form mixture into a ball. Press dough into a flat circle. On a lightly floured board, roll out dough to 13" x 9". Carefully press dough into bottom of foil-lined pan. Prick dough every 2 to 3 inches with a fork. Bake in preheated oven 8 to 10 minutes or until dough is firm but not brown. Reduce oven temperature to 350F(175C). Meanwhile, using an electric mixer in a large bowl, beat cream cheese, eggs and goat cheese until smooth. Stir in tomatoes, marjoram, fine herbs, salt and half and half. Pour over hot crust. Return pan to oven. Bake 18 to 20 minutes or until firm. Cool on a wire rack. When cool, lift out of pan; remove foil. Cut into 2 (13" x 4-1/2") rectangles. Place each on a serving tray. With dull side of a large knife, score tops diagonally about 1- to 1-1/2-inches apart. Fill each row with a different garnish; see suggested garnishes below. Cut into 1-1/2-inch bars. Makes 40 to 48 bars.

Garnishes:

Sliced ripe olives
Sliced green onions
Black or golden caviar

Chopped hard-cooked egg
Chopped red or green bell pepper

Tic-Tac-Toe Twists

Novel shapes and great flavors make these rolls a favorite with everyone.

1 cup all-purpose flour
1/4 teaspoon dried leaf basil, crushed
1/4 teaspoon dried leaf oregano, crushed
1/8 teaspoon seasoned pepper
1/8 teaspoon garlic salt

1/2 cup butter or margarine
1/2 cup (2 oz.) shredded mozzarella cheese
1/4 cup (3/4 oz.) grated Parmesan cheese
3 to 3-1/2 tablespoons cold water

Preheat oven to 425F (220C). In a medium bowl, combine flour, basil, oregano, seasoned pepper and garlic salt. Add butter; with a pastry blender or fork, cut in butter until mixture resembles coarse crumbs. Stir in mozzarella and Parmesan cheese. Sprinkle 1 tablespoon water at a time over mixture, stirring with a fork until all flour is moistened. Divide dough into 12 pieces. On a lightly floured board, use your fingers to roll each piece of dough into a 15-inch rope. Divide 6 ropes into 4 (3-3/4-inch) pieces. Cross 2 pieces to form an "X". Repeat with remaining 3-3/4-inch pieces. Divide each of remaining 6 (15-inch) ropes in half. Form each half into a circle on a large baking sheet. Bake in preheated oven 8 to 11 minutes or until golden brown. Makes 24 pieces.

Finger Foods Designed for Celebrations

*Make your favorite special event more memorable for family or
friends by featuring one or more of these celebration recipes along
with your favorite party foods.*

Valentine's Day

Lattice Almond-Berry Heart
Red-Hot Popcorn Heart
Snowcap Raspberry Finger-Puffs

St. Patrick's Day

Layered Pesto Spread
Chocolate-Mint Sandwiches

Wedding Showers or Receptions

Open-Faced Salmon-Caper Sandwiches
Savory Goat-Cheese Bars
Herbed Party Sandwiches
Layered Pesto Spread
Cold Meat Party Carousel

Anniversary Celebrations

Crab-Stuffed Artichoke Bottoms
Caviar-Topped Filo Cups
Tic-Tac-Toe Twists
Hazelnut Tarts with Raspberry Glaze

Celebration Tea

Seashell Madeleine Cookies
Herbed Party Sandwiches
Open-Faced Salmon-Caper Sandwiches
Hazelnut Tarts with Raspberry Glaze
Tropical Stacks
Double Chocolate-Pecan Treats

Halloween

Chocolate-Meringue Pumpkin Faces
Nacho Cheese Pita Jack-O'-Lanterns

Christmas

Spicy Holiday Thumbprints
New Zealand Fruitcake Squares
Glazed Holiday Fruit Bars
Orange-Mincemeat Loaf
Cranberry-White-Chocolate Cereal Bars
Layered Pesto Spread
Chocolate-Mint Sandwiches

Metric Chart

Comparison to Metric Measure

When You Know	Symbol	Multiply By	To Find	Symbol
teaspoons	tsp	5.0	milliliters	ml
tablespoons	tbsp	15.0	milliliters	ml
fluid ounces	fl. oz.	30.0	milliliters	ml
cups	c	0.24	liters	l
pints	pt.	0.47	liters	l
quarts	qt.	0.95	liters	l
ounces	oz.	28.0	grams	g
pounds	lb.	0.45	kilograms	kg
Fahrenheit	F	5/9 (after subtracting 32)	Celsius	C

Liquid Measure to Milliliters

1/4 teaspoon	=	1.25 milliliters
1/2 teaspoon	=	2.5 milliliters
3/4 teaspoon	=	3.75 milliliters
1 teaspoon	=	5.0 milliliters
1-1/4 teaspoons	=	6.25 milliliters
1-1/2 teaspoons	=	7.5 milliliters
1-3/4 teaspoons	=	8.75 milliliters
2 teaspoons	=	10.0 milliliters
1 tablespoon	=	15.0 milliliters
2 tablespoons	=	30.0 milliliters

Fahrenheit to Celsius

F	C
200—205	95
220—225	105
245—250	120
275	135
300—305	150
325—330	165
345—350	175
370—375	190
400—405	205
425—430	220
445—450	230
470—475	245
500	260

Liquid Measure to Liters

1/4 cup	=	0.06 liters
1/2 cup	=	0.12 liters
3/4 cup	=	0.18 liters
1 cup	=	0.24 liters
1-1/4 cups	=	0.3 liters
1-1/2 cups	=	0.36 liters
2 cups	=	0.48 liters
2-1/2 cups	=	0.6 liters
3 cups	=	0.72 liters
3-1/2 cups	=	0.84 liters
4 cups	=	0.96 liters
4-1/2 cups	=	1.08 liters
5 cups	=	1.2 liters
5-1/2 cups	=	1.32 liters

Index